NORWIC[

Stock No.

D1322677

Class

Cat. | M | Proc. | SWCC

RUGBY COACHING
THE NEW ZEALAND WAY

by
RODNEY BUTT

ICENI
BOOKS

199 341

Rugby Coaching the New Zealand Way

All Rights Reserved.
Copyright © 2003 Rodney Butt (roddybutt@hotmail.com)

No part of this book may be reproduced or retransmitted in any form or by any means without the written permission of the publisher.

International Standard Book Number:
1-58736-182-5
Library of Congress Control Number:
2003100259

Published by Iceni Books™
610 East Delano Street, Suite 104
Tucson, Arizona 85705 U.S.A.
www.icenibooks.com

TABLE OF CONTENTS

FOREWORD

The day you stop learning is the day you die. Rugby is no exception, as you are constantly learning new ways to be a better player or coach. The game changes every year as professional teams come up with new ways to be successful, trying to get the edge on their opponents. From an early age I knew I wanted to coach rugby, and after learning something new, I would go home after training and write it down. I still refer to those notes, many of which are part of this book. It is amazing how much you can forget if you do not write it down.

I was lucky to have All Black back coach and Canterbury Crusaders coach Robbie Deans coach me for three years with Canterbury Country. With the Canterbury Colts, my coach was Des Hansen, who is the father of Canterbury and Wales coach Steve Hansen. Canterbury Crusaders forward coach and former Canterbury captain Don Hayes was another outstanding source of knowledge under whom I was lucky enough to play. Coaching is an art form, and you can learn a lot of good things from coaches of other sports. My cousin, Adam Gardner, is a professional tennis coach in China. He told me of a thirty-second rule he has during training, whereby he will stop and talk for no more than thirty seconds at a time as players get cold. Also, importantly, players can only take in a certain amount of information at one time. This is a good rule, regardless of what sport you coach, but it's especially a good rule for an outdoor winter game like rugby. In 1994 I was given an opportunity to trial for the Western Reds rugby league side in Perth, Western Australia. I secured a contract and trained as a professional when rugby was still an amateur game. Training everyday opened my eyes to variety training, weight training, sprint training, and skill work. Also, running in sand and swimming were a part of our regime. After two years of league, I returned to rugby and was lucky enough to finish my career playing and traveling in some interesting parts of the world. I spent a season in England and a season in Canada, as well as playing on and coaching a tens team in Malaysia and club rugby in Japan, where I am now a full-time rugby coach. Rugby has been good to me, and it is an excellent way to see the world, as rugby clubs in any country share a warmth and you always get good hospitality. You instantly become part of the family there and you make many lifelong friends whom you would not meet if you were just a tourist or traveler. Of course life is not perfect and you hear of the odd bad experience. I had mine in Italy at a club called Liverno, which promised plenty. One door closes and another opens, so I went to England and had a good season.

In New Zealand I was lucky enough to play with or against the All Blacks, Andrew Mertens, Leon McDonald, Carlos Spencer, Graham Bachop, Mark Hammet, Robbie Deans, Darryl Gibson, and Todd Blackadder. While in Perth I completed a sports psychology diploma, mainly because I realised the importance of having your mind and your body at their best in order to play well.

Also, motivation is a big part of being a good captain or coach of a rugby side at any level. In 2002 I coached one of Canterbury's top club sides, Christchurch, into third place. At thirty-four, I am still a young coach and am learning, but I am sure there is something in this book for you.

I would like to thank Leigh Ayers for her great help, and I dedicate this book to all the players and coaches I have been lucky enough to meet, sweat with, learn from, and drink some beer with, such as coaches like Mike Ryan, Noel Hickland, Bob Kerr, Craig Hale, Don Hayes, and players like Okie Myberg, Mark Cohoon, Clint Ford, Ian Shinn, and Big Ray Sharp. Please enjoy.

FAMOUS QUOTES AND SAYINGS

Success is more a function of consistent common sense than it is of genius.

Without struggle there is no progress.

I don't expect you to be the best, just the best you can be.

When looking for a hand, you will find one at the end of your arm.

You can't learn anything while you are talking.

Minds are like parachutes. They only function when they are open.

After all is said and done, there is more said than done.

Even if you are on the right track, you will get run over if you stand still.

Everybody dies, but few people live.

We are all kings, but we don't wear crowns.

I never lose, but I have been behind when time ran out.

To be old and wise, first you must be young and stupid.

If you don't like my cooking, lower your standards.

The dictionary is the only place where success comes before work.

The only thing worse than carrying on is failure.

Reach for the stars, but keep your feet on the ground.

It's nice to be important, but it's more important to be nice.

Win without boasting, lose without excuse.

Growing old is inevitable, growing up is optional.

A rich person is not who has the most, but who needs the least.

Put the chocolate down and no one will get hurt.

If we are what we eat, I'm either fast, cheap, or easy.

They say one in four people is mentally imbalanced. Think of three friends, and if they seem normal, then you are the one.

You can't make an omelette without breaking eggs.

Work as if you don't need the money; love as if you've never been hurt; dance as if nobody's watching.

I have never known a dream to go anywhere on its own.

There is no such thing as a great talent without great willpower.

I would rather be an opportunist and float, than go to the bottom with my principles around my neck.

A celebrity is a person who works hard all his life to become known, then wears dark glasses to avoid being recognised.

It's not the men in my life that counts, it's the life in my men. — Mae West

Take care to get what you like or you will be forced to like what you get.

Be nice to people on your way up because you will meet them again on your way down.

I never forget a face, but in your case I will be glad to make an exception.

If a man hasn't discovered something he will die for, he isn't fit to live. — Martin Luther King, Jr.

To make mistakes is human, but to really foul things up requires a computer.

There is no heavier burden than unfulfilled potential.

No one can make you feel inferior without your consent.

The greatest mistake you can make in life is to be constantly fearing you will make one.

Some people are always grumbling that roses have thorns; be thankful that thorns have roses.

Happiness is not having what you want, but wanting what you have.

I have got a great ambition to die of exhaustion rather than boredom.

The fragrance always stays in the hand that fives the rose.

When money is at stake, never be the first to mention sums.

If you want a place in the sun, you've got to put up with a few blisters.

The worst mistake a boss can make is not to say, "Well done."

Always do your best. What you plant now, you will harvest later.

If you see a bandwagon, it's too late.

Workaholics commit slow suicide by refusing to allow the child inside them to play.

When you are getting kicked from the rear, it means that you are in front.

The proverb warns that "you should not bite the hand that feeds you," but maybe you should if it prevents you from feeding yourself.

Anxiety is the interest paid on trouble before it is due.

Turn to the sports pages first, which records people's accomplishments. The front page has nothing but man's failures.

Opera is when a guy gets stabbed in the back and, instead of bleeding, he sings.

The race is long, and in the end it is only with yourself.

Success is the result of good judgement, good judgement is the result of experience, and experience is often the result of bad judgement.

Sometimes you have to be in the dark to see the light. Sometimes you must be down before getting up to fight.

Trophies are a by-product of a good performance. — John Mitchell.

Habit is either the best of servants or the worst of masters.

Do not look for a hero. Be one.

If you cannot face the music, you will never lead the band.

BECOMING A GREAT PLAYER

Aim high. You must have a goal to aim for. Have you ever tried archery blindfolded? It is tough if you cannot see or do not have a target to aim at. Work hard towards your goal. If you are a lazy trainer, get over it. Otherwise there will be someone else down the road who is prepared to do what you are not. Admit your weaknesses and work on them. Learn the skills required for your position and constantly fine-tune them. Add to them with more skills to help you on your way to becoming a great player. These days, forwards can run and pass like backs, and backs are now tackling harder and learning forward's skills at ruck and maul time. You cannot be too skillful or knowledgeable about any facet of the game.

Where do great players come from? Some successful sports people started their respective sports early. For example, Andre Agassi, Tiger Woods, Martina Hingis, and (I believe) Christian Cullen were all very focused on their prospective sports from a young age. However, there are just as many who were not as naturally gifted and who developed into champions. Michael Jordan is a good example; he didn't make his school basketball team on his first try. He turned out all right though, didn't he? What about Babe Ruth? He was definitely not a natural athlete and had a few slumps on his way to immortality. He held the world record for strike-outs as well as the record for home runs. It is better to try and fail than to not try at all.

Back to our four champions. Agassi, Cullen, Hingis, and Woods were all coached from an early age and remained a couple of lengths ahead of their rivals. Christian Cullen, he's awesome! His strength training was evident early on when his bench press ability made the gossip rounds of

New Zealand rugby when he first made the Wellington squad. Sprint training is strongly recommended for players of all positions these days, but Cullen's acceleration would be tough to coach into any player. Off the field I have never heard a bad word about the guy, and I understand he is a 100% good bloke. From the outside looking in, it appears Hingis and Agassi may have been pushed a little into their sports. Andre has been up and down more times than Bill Clinton, but you have to take your hat off to one of the greats when he is at his best.

Martina Hingis looks to be having a good time when she plays tennis, which I am sure contributes to her outstanding success. Hingis found the power games of Davenport and the Williams sisters a little tough, but who wouldn't? Unfortunately, she lost a lot of friends after her infamous loss to Steffi Graff. There was not a lot of Sean Fitzpatrick-type after-match sportsmanship that day. Perhaps the pressure of her mother being coach, sports psychologist, friend, and parent all came to a head. Do you think if she were Colin Meads's or Brian Lochore's daughter, she might have got a kick up the backside that day? (No offense, legends!) I hope she is not remembered for that game over and above her great career.

To my mind, Tiger Woods is the ultimate sportsman. He has the strength and fitness, and he is focused and so diplomatic. He realises how hard it is to constantly fire on all cylinders; therefore he lets himself cruise a little, then he explodes into the majors. Sure, he was strongly encouraged by his parents to play golf, but they also instilled sportsmanship and values, which shine through.

So in summary, you should be serious about your sport, eat the right foods, and rehydrate. Do the speed, strength, ball skills, and flexibility training. Get the coaching and constantly look to learn. Work on weaknesses, and maybe you will be a great player, or at least you will not die wondering. Good luck.

Advanced Coaching Tips

Be honest with your players and be responsible. Be well organised and passionate about the game. It helps to be consistent as to what time training starts and finishes. Do not be too domineering, as all the players have a voice also. Try to do most of your talking before training. Your players cannot be too skillful or flexible, so incorporate plenty of skill drills and stretching.

Give players prior notice if they are to be dropped; this is much more professional than just announcing the team. You need to give constructive feedback to the dropped player; he will appreciate this. Be approachable. Players need to feel comfortable with discussing any problems they may have, on or off the field, and be able to have you treat them in confidence. Let players try other playing positions if they want to. A coach must be flexible with this. Remember, positions are just numbers on backs, and the game must be enjoyable for all. Encourage involvement. A player cannot be caught out of position if his side has the ball. Too many players run back to their position while play is still going, and they find themselves too far away from play. Do not be afraid to seek help, as no one knows all positional requirements, and players will respect you more if you do not try to do everything yourself. Successful people ask the right questions and get good answers.

One way of giving the players responsibility is to ask them every three or four weeks how they played, both personally and as a team, in their last game. In an open discussion with players and coaching staff, a player is likely to be honest and realise areas that need improvement. This takes a lot of pressure off the coach because criticism is not coming from him. However, remember that any criticism should be constructive with a positive outcome.

They say that variety is the spice of life, so incorporate plenty of it when planning training exercises. Boxing, swimming, hockey, basketball, tennis, track and field, squash, rugby league, netball, Aussie rules, baseball, and soccer can be stimulating for a change. Coaches are only limited by their imagination. Always look to improve.

A coach of the L.A. Lakers wondered how he could get the champion team to improve and not rest on its laurels. He asked each player to improve by only one percent in five areas of his game. Each player had to name the areas and be responsible for his own progress. Only one percent seemed very achievable and was; however, collectively the team improved immensely and took all the silverware that season.

Most young players are not good distributors, especially if they are strong runners themselves! For them to get anywhere, they must learn how and when to give the pass to their teammate. Having the awareness to sum up the options and unload if a fellow player is in a better position to continue the movement is a skill in itself. This is called *vision*. It does not matter how fit a player is; if she or he is running around in circles, they are of little value. Players must learn or be taught what lines to run, with or without the ball. Michael Jones and Josh Kronfield were very good at predicting where the breakdown would take place so they could get there and help secure possession for their side. In support, it is important to keep some depth, as too many players are too flat and put themselves offside because they overrun the ball carrier. If the support player has depth, the ball carrier has the option of passing to his/her left or right, before or after contact. Also, the support player can go in and help to maintain the ball from behind.

Wayne Gretzey of Brantford in Canada was the greatest ice hockey player of all time. In North America, he is known as "The Great One." Once a reporter asked him,

"Why are you the best? You are not the biggest, not the strongest, and you are not the fastest player on ice." Wayne Gretzey replied, "Most people skate to where the puck is. I skate to where the puck is going." This is vision!

GOAL KICKING

Practice! Head down! Rhythm! If you are a novice goal kicker or if your form is not as good as it could be, then you go back to basics. Get plenty of practice off a short run-up, from just one or two steps, to get a feel for the ball coming off your foot correctly. Then you can extend your run-up but still focus on your timing and consistency without too much power. If you continue to hit the ball well, you can always increase your power. You should look to kick the ball the same way each time with the same pre-kick routine. You should take the same amount of steps back—and forward—on your approach to the ball. Most people now like to lean the ball forward, which helps to find a sweet spot on the bottom end of the ball. It also helps the ball to fly straight without too much curl or swing. The kick itself should be no different, whether you like to stand the ball up straight or lean it forward. Do most of your practicing in front of the posts; this will help you to find a rhythm without trying to kick the skin off the ball. Do not be too stiff on your approach. It is better to be relaxed, on your toes, and taking small steps. Do not be nervous. Stay loose and confident.

The reason everybody tells you to keep your head down is because your leg will come through much straighter. Try this standing still and see how much further your leg will swing sideways if you lift your head. So keep your head down and do not look up too early to see where the ball has gone. The damage is already done. If you are a right footer, and you are missing to the left or curling too much, you can almost guarantee you are lifting your head too soon. Former All Black Robbie Deans believes you should only look up in time to see the touch judge's flags go up. If you look up before that, then you are lifting your head too soon. If you are a right footer and you are missing to the right of the posts, then chances are that your left or plant foot is too far away from the ball on contact. It's just like golf. Practice, head down, and rhythm. Golfing great Jack Nicklaus would imagine a successful golf shot just before he played one. He would have visions of the ball landing where he wanted it to. Then he would work his way back from there, imagining the ball sailing through the air, then leaving his club face from a smooth swing. He would then go about producing a good shot after he had just been through it in his mind. That's worth some thought, goal kickers!

Daryl Halligan, All Black kicking coach and record points scorer in rugby league, on goal kicking. The key basics are:

- Have your kickers develop a positive attitude. If talking to kickers about kicking, then talk about the successes they have experienced (e.g., goals kicked in the past). They should see themselves as successful goal kickers.

- Then the goal kickers must take that confidence from the training paddock. They must put the time into practice. Start with simple goals from in front: twenty-five metres out, then thirty-five metres. Kick twenty-five to thirty-five kicks per session with no more than thirty-five metres on any angle to engender a high (80% or more) success level.

- The more difficult kicks will fall into place if this basis has been laid. By kicking these close goals and achieving 80%-plus success in training, the kicker will complement his/her visualization by actions that reinforce it.

TECHNIQUES

Although some aspects of technique are individual, there are some basics to keep in mind.

1. Make sure you are as upright as possible and are over the top of the ball when striking the kick.
2. Having your opposite shoulder upright and tall helps your body to be over the top of the ball.
3. The run-up varies according to each kicker, but it should be balanced and lead to techniques one and two, discussed above.

COACHES

Kickers need help to visualise themselves succeeding. Do this three or four times after placing the ball and before kicking it. This visualization is the most important element, along with positive thinking, for successful goal kicking. You need to set goal-kicking tasks in a proactive consideration of the percentage of success wanted in a game, e.g., 80%-plus in front of the posts. Treat those to the side as a bonus. Look for potential kickers in players who have natural timing in their kicking. Have your kickers warm up before a game with a few kicks. This will help them focus.

Andrew Mertens, All Black points-scoring record holder, on goal kicking.

- Expose the sweet spot of the ball.
- Align the ball with the target.
- Move back.
- Approach in an arc.
- Turn shoulder in.
- Plant non-kicking foot.
- Swing through the strike zone.

BEING DROPPED

We have all been there. It does not matter who you are or how good you might be. If you have not been dropped yet, sometime in the future you will be. The question is, how should you react and turn this into a positive?

First, the onus should be on the non-selected player to congratulate the player selected for his position. It may be difficult, but you will earn a lot of respect from the other players and the coach. Do not worry about your bruised ego. Team unity and friendship are more important. In your own mind, nullify the intensity of the situation. Change words like "depressed" to "challenged," "stressed out" to "recharging." Do not beat yourself up. What does not kill you will make you stronger! Find a strategy to make yourself better. Do not spit the dummy. Instead, ask your coach where you can improve. Also, look at it from his point of view. Additionally, if you get the chance to play off the bench or for the team below, explode. Play out of your skin to prove a point. Soft players will still be feeling sorry for themselves while you will be on your way back in. You cannot change the past, so look to the future. Also, think of your strong points. Have no anxiety because you are still a capable and valued person.

Now back to congratulating the selected player. This reminds me of the All Black great Buck Shelford who was somehow dropped after never losing a game as the All Black captain. It caused an uproar in New Zealand rugby circles when he was replaced by a young number eight in Zinzan Brooke. Later, of course, Brooke turned out to be a great, but at the time he was selected, it was mainly because he belonged to a dominant Auckland side. Buck Shelford rang Brooke to personally congratulate him on his

All Black selection. It must have been extremely hard for him to make that call. He wasn't just a great All Black captain and player, but a great man.

THE PERFECT PLAYER

If there is such a thing as a perfect player, in my mind, he or she would have nine attributes. I will name them and then break them up individually. They may help you realise your weak and strong points.

They are: discipline, skills, determination, motivation, rugby intelligence, self-confidence, personality, concentration, and communication.

DISCIPLINE

- Train hard for physical fitness, strength, etc.
- Eat right.
- Must play within the rules of the game.
- Penalties will kill any team.
- Accept referees' decisions without talking back.
- Don't spit the dummy.
- Accept coaches decisions even if you do not always agree.

SKILLS

- Should have obvious ability to perform the skills required in the game.
- Skills should be learnt and constantly fine-tuned. Once mastered, they should be performed consistently with the right techniques.

DETERMINATION

This quality speaks for itself.
- Fight to succeed.

- Don't give up.
- Be competitive.
- Have the will to win.
- Work hard.
- Have guts.
- Break the pain barrier.

MOTIVATION

- Want to succeed.
- Do it for yourself and your teammates.
- Have goals, aims, and desire.
- Strive and have inspiration.

RUGBY INTELLIGENCE

- Possess knowledge of the game.
- Know more than your rivals.
- Be proactive.
- Do the little things right.
- Have the ability to read the game.

SELF-CONFIDENCE.

- Be your best.
- Believe you are anyone's equal.
- You can deal with any problems that may arise.
- Remain cool and confident.
- Belief is the mother of reality.

PERSONALITY

- Have character, power from within, and personal pride.
- Be a hard worker. Never lay down.
- Have guts and the ability to be honest with yourself and others.

- Be able to work alongside others.
- Respect others' opinions.
- Be a team person.

CONCENTRATION

- Be able to switch on for the whole game.
- Focus on the moment; don't leave it on the training paddock.
- Put it all together.
- Perform.
- Have the ability to learn and retain.
- Apply yourself.

COMMUNICATION

- Loud calling for the ball.
- Don't go quiet during the game.
- Talk to teammates on and off the field.
- Be positive.

It would be wrong to suggest that any one player could possess all the above attributes and apply them perfectly. But imagine the potential of a team of rugby players that, between all the players, possesses, retains, and applies the attributes listed. What an awesome team! The possibilities would be endless!

KICKING

THE SPIRAL PUNT

This is probably the longest of kicks. The most important aspect of this is consistency because so often the ball can come off the side of the foot and be a shocker. Try to place the ball as close to your foot as possible, in contrast to throwing the ball too soon where it can shift or float before contact. Practice this with little or no power and feel the ball rolling or spiralling off your foot. Keep your toe pointed out and try to kick through the ball in a straight line.

The spiral should come from the ball rolling off your foot, not from swinging your whole leg sideways. Much like golf, it is your timing and consistency that counts, so do not try to always kick the hell out of it.

If the opposition's open-side winger is up flat and their fullback is hugging the middle of the field, then a long spiral wipers or raking kick can result in a major territorial gain. This is best done by your number ten or twelve. If your inside centre or second five-eight does the kick, then their backs, including their open-side wing, will be rushing up. This will result in them having to turn and a easier chase for your backline.

UP AND UNDER OR BOMB

This is not used as much as it used to be, mainly because sides are less reluctant to give away possession, but it is still a useful option. The kick over the scrum or line-out by your scrum-half works well to isolate their blindside winger. A good kick and a good chase can result with your line-out throw after bustling their winger into touch. This works well if you are in your own half but outside your twenty-two. The scrum-half or halfback should take a big step back to give himself room before kicking over the top. The ball should be kicked on the end for more height and accuracy.

A good play when your fly-half or first five-eight is putting up a high kick was used a lot by former Welsh international and British Lion Jonathan Davies. When he got the ball, he would run to the open side and dummy cut or dummy switch with his inside centre. This would stop the opposition's flanker and bring their backs rushing up. After the dummy, he would then kick a high ball where their fullback was isolated, with plenty of chasers coming through. This works best when running to the right so the right foot can be used for the high kick. This can also be used for the grubber or chip kick. It is effective because it commits their backs to rush up, putting them out of play if the kick goes behind them and because the kick is made close to the tackle or gain line.

THE DROP KICK

The most important aspect of the drop kick is the position of the ball on contact. It should be just touching the ground, and standing straight up. If you can get this part right consistently, you are almost there. Too often the ball falls sideways when it hits the ground, generally to the right if you are a right-foot kicker. So be conscious of this when dropping the ball, and even lean it in slightly. After this it becomes a timing thing, trying to kick the ball just as it hits the ground and no later. If you are desiring a higher kick from a restart, delay your contact to enable you to get under the ball, which will result in more height. Otherwise it should still be the same kick with a good straight follow-through, much like a place kick. Do not swing the leg sideways too much, but keep a straight line through the ball, pointing in the desired direction of landing. Another common problem area is dropping the ball from too high up, which enables the ball to deviate or float around too much. Therefore, starting and keeping the ball low down and close to your foot is a better technique to produce the desired results.

THE DROP-PUNT

Aussie rules style. This is also used often by rugby league players and is starting to be used in rugby union. Andrew Mertens, Carlos Spencer, and former league player Andrew Walker are not afraid to adopt this style when kicking for touch. It is very accurate with little chance of the ball coming off the side of the foot. The ball is best held low and pointing downwards. A straight leg action makes contact with the bottom or just above the bottom of the ball. It is very important to keep your head down. Once you have mastered the drop-punt, the ball should fly very straight. The experts of this style, namely Aussie rules players, can swing the ball both ways, unlike the spiral kick which generally curls to the left for right footers. These Aussie rules players can also kick long distances with great precision.

If you are a young first five-eight or fly-half, the drop-punt is a good skill to learn to help your kicking game.

COACHES' PRE-GAME TALKS

Be positive on match day. No anxiety or pressure. Build confidence so the team can explode into action. Do not focus on the opposition. They just happen to be the team that you are giving it to this week. Talk of how you are going to out-run, out-jump, out-tackle, out-scrum, and basically about how you intend to blow them away. Sure, it may be a tough game or a hard afternoon, where a lot of effort is required, but your team is more likely to play like the All Blacks if you tell them they *are* the All Blacks. Tell them they are anyone's equal and that you are proud to coach them. That the hairs on the back of your neck will stand up when the team takes the field and that they are not alone. Do not say *win, win, win* (that's pressure). Instead, tell them how and why they are going to win and what tactics will help them succeed.

Some people have different opinions about rating the opposition. I am a firm believer in being arrogant and that it is better to have no respect for them. Sure, you can be too cocky, if you are not prepared to work, but I think too many coaches put their own teams on the back foot by building up the opposition. A coach once told our team before the match to go wide all day because our forwards were going to be out-played. It may have been on the cards that this might happen, but that sort of talk does nothing for team morale or confidence building, especially in the forward pack.

Think of France versus New Zealand, World Cup, 1999. All the talk from the New Zealand coach was how unpredictable the French are and how good they can be. The French ran onto the paddock believing in themselves and believing they could win. They were probably listening to what the All Black coach was saying about them! The All Blacks were not ruthless and were wary of the opposition.

Why do some teams have a much better record of wins at home, as opposed to at away games? It is just another rugby field and it is the same for both teams. People say it is the local crowd or support, but a player should be focused totally on the game, and not the sideline anyway. I think it is a mental thing, as players do not feel as comfortable or as confident in a different surrounding.

A good approach is to tell your team that you are all travelling to stake a marker on the opposition's turf as a group of rugby players out to prove your rugby playing ability together.

On a wet day, tell your team that any day is a good day to play rugby. Any day is a good day to put on this jersey and play with your mates. Say it is easier to beat guys in the mud, as the opposition cannot turn quickly or react fast. The wet ground evens everyone up and the team who wants it more will win.

Last man standing.

VISUALISATION

What is it that makes a person a winner? What distinguishes those who succeed from those who fail? "It's all in the mind," says movie star and bodybuilder Arnold Schwarzenegger. A multi-millionaire, successful real estate tycoon, movie star, bodybuilder, five-time winner of Mr. Universe, Arnold has made it. But it wasn't always so!

Arnold can remember back when he had nothing except a belief that his mind was the key to getting where he wanted to go. "When I was very young, I visualised myself being and having what I wanted. Mentally, I never had any doubts about it. The mind is incredible. Before I won my first Mr. Universe, I walked around the tournament like I owned it. The title was already mine. I had won it so many times in my mind that there was no doubt I would win it. When I moved on to the movies with the same pattern, I visualised myself being a successful actor and earning big money. I could feel and taste the success. I just knew it would all happen."

Chris Poellein was a member of the world-renowned West German freestyle ski team which won the European Cup six times between 1976 and 1982. "Part of our training involved working with the psychologist to increase the power of our minds. After training on the slopes, we were placed in a state of meditation and encouraged to totally repeat the slope runs in our minds, visualizing each bump and movement to the routine. We worked as hard training mentally as we did physically. Excellence in athletics—or indeed in any endeavour—depends primarily on having a clear mental picture of that activity."

All Black great Michael Jones would go through a game of rugby in his mind before game day. He pictured himself running good lines and angles, taking good options in certain situations that could arise. Sometimes he would do this while jogging on an empty rugby field. If you have already been over it in your mind, when a tough decision arrives, your subconscious will help you take the right option. Playing experience will do the same thing to help skills and tactics become second nature. You can also train your nervous system to perform a skill consistently well. The Boston Celtics great Larry Bird was once asked to miss a shot from the free-throw line during the filming of a soft-drink commercial. It took him nine successful shots to bring himself to miss one basket. His subconscious and nervous system were so used to making the shot. Johnny Wilkinson, Andrew Mertens, and Neil Jenkins may have got close to this skill level with their goal kicking.

MAINTAINING FITNESS LEVELS

WHAT KIND OF TRAINING
SHOULD YOU DO?

We recommend you get a balance of the four "S"s: suppleness, stamina, strength, and speed are the main components of off-season training. Having the right mix of these elements will ensure that you have a happy season. Suppleness, or flexibility, is an extremely important part of any training programme and everyday life. Suppleness will help keep you injury-free and make most everyday activities easier to achieve. The best time for your flexibility training is when the body is warm, e.g., after a workout. Stretching can be done anywhere, anytime, provided you have done a warm-up.

Stamina training builds up the aerobic fitness you will need to last the whole game. This can be something as simple as a half-hour run or a mountain bike ride in the hills. Try taking part in activities you would not normally do during the season.

Strength training will ensure that your muscles stand up to the strain they are put under in today's game. Strength gains are made through resistance work, such as weight training. Recent research has shown that resistance training also increases bone density. Strength training is very important for all-over health benefits. The off-season is the perfect time to make a start on strength training if you are not doing it already.

Speed training is not as important as these others during the off-season, but it really helps during pre-season training. Speed training helps with those short sprints that you will need during the game.

How often should I train?

Having the right mix of the four "S"s means that you will get the results that you need. You could try the following programme:

- Suppleness — every session
- Stamina — three sessions per week
- Strength — three sessions per week
- Speed — optional

Make your training as much fun as possible. This is your big chance to try something different, such as circuit training, aerobics, cycling, or perhaps swimming. There are many options out there, so add variety and make your programme interesting. Remember, off-season training helps you start the season like a champion. It can be a heap of fun, and you will really enjoy the change in a training routine. Robbie Deans believes off-season is where an individual can gain the edge.

THE COUNTERATTACK

There are two types of counterattack. One occurs after you have created a turnover, and the other is after the ball has been kicked to your team, usually to your back three, full-back and wingers. Turnover ball is fast becoming one of the best opportunities to attack from. It is normally a quick ball, so try and keep it that way and move the ball to space quickly. Do not have any forwards or runners taking the ball up to set up another faze. Give the backs their chance to best use the element of surprise. If defence has quickly become attack, then the opposition's defensive line will be unorganised and vulnerable. This will happen especially out wide where their outside backs are at depth, waiting to receive the ball; therefore, they have a bit of ground to cover to reach the gain line or tackle line.

The other counterattack option comes after fielding a kick — but not every kick. Christian Cullen has taken this to a new level with his individual talent of beating the first few chasers or defenders. Not everyone has the ability to run the ball back effectively on their own, so your option-taking needs to be carefully considered. You will soon become unpopular with your teammates if you have a habit of getting caught a long way behind the advantage or gain line. No one likes having to run backwards, especially big forwards. This is a simple but effective strategy to use, especially if you are new to playing wing or fullback.

Only counterattack if you have received a bad kick. A good tactical kick by the opposition would not give you the necessary space to implement a successful counterattack. Also, you need time for your support to arrive back to help you. When you retrieve the ball with time and space, look to run for about eight metres directly back to where the ball was kicked from. This will freeze the opposition initially, giving you time to decide whether to run, pass, or kick the ball. If you run directly to the open side or to space, then the opposition will slide across and your counterattack will face more defenders. They will not slide as quickly if you appear to be running straight at them for those first few strides. This also enables your support to line up outside of you with some space.

If the blindside winger receives a kick with time, he should pass the ball quickly in field to his fullback, especially if the winger is close to the touchline. Because the sideline restricts space, the fullback has more options open to him or her. He can run or pass left or right. If the counterattack is on, then he can link up with the other members of your backline on the open side. The high kick is always an option, and the chip-over is a dangerous but sometimes awarding alternative.

TEAM SPIRIT

To be successful, a good team spirit is essential. It starts with the coach and the senior players welcoming new squad members with open arms. First impressions are important in helping a new player to feel comfortable and fit in. Players need to be good mates on and off the field. Solidarity and loyalty to each other are important. Keep reserves involved as much as possible. They should be cheering on teammates and congratulating them after a win and vice versa when their turn comes to take the field. They all have to throw their hats into the ring, regardless of background, experience, and culture to work together when they take the field. Coaches can help by being approachable at any time for a one-on-one chat. A coach should always be honest and should not embarrass players in public. Everyone should have a voice.

Players, coaches, medical staff, and managers should all have faith in one another. It is a good idea early in the season to have a good night out as a team so everyone can relax a little and get to know each other better. Players' partners should be encouraged also to support the team players and meet others at the rugby club. This will also take some pressure off the player who might otherwise be expected to rush home after games sometimes. Doing an adventure course is very good to help players to work as a team.

NUTRITIONAL AWARENESS

When you increase your exercise intensity, this has to be met nutritionally to provide you with energy to perform. To help us eat the right foods for our body, we need to have knowledge of the effects food has. This is best described in the breakdown of foods into major nutrients, i.e., carbohydrates, proteins, fats, water, dietary fibre, vitamins and minerals. When we exercise, our body needs fuel to perform, and the major fuel is glucose. Glucose is stored in the muscles and liver in the form of glycogen. This is a related compound that is readily converted into glucose, as needed for energy. The amount of glycogen available to the muscles is the key factor in how much activity you can perform without becoming physically tired. Carbohydrates are the main source of energy in the diet because these compounds are quickly converted into glycogen. There are two types of carbohydrates: simple and complex.

SIMPLE CARBOHYDRATES

The simple carbohydrates are sugars. They are small molecules that are easily digested to provide instant energy to the muscles. This type of energy, however, is short lived as it provides a sudden boost of glucose to the bloodstream, giving energy. Then about twenty minutes later, there is a sudden drop, which can leave you feeling weak and shaky and result in low performance. However, a little fruit juice in water taken constantly in endurance events can provide instantly needed energy. It is not recommended to base your diet around the simple sugars.

COMPLEX CARBOHYDRATES

It is best to consume complex carbohydrates (starches) such as cereals, grains (wholemeal, unrefined), i.e., bread rolls, crackers, pasta, rice, and legumes (beans and peas). These foods provide longer-lasting energy, as they are more complex molecules. When they breakdown, the unused carbohydrates are stored as glycogen to provide energy when needed.

FATS

The second source of energy after glucose is used up is found in stored fatty acids. The beneficial fats to consume are the vegetable fats: olive oil, flaxseed oil, canola oil, safflower oil, and sunflower oil. The oils are only beneficial to the body unheated: cold on salads or poured over food and kept stored in dark glass bottles. Other beneficial fats include fish, nuts, and seeds. Consume dairy products, such as yoghurt, cheese, and milk, in moderation.

PROTEINS

The preferred protein foods to consume are, in order, fish, tofu, chicken, red meat (lean quality cuts), legumes, nuts, seeds, and dairy. Proteins are needed to build muscle, for tissue repair, and for the production of enzymes used in digestion.

WATER

The most essential nutrient. Water in everyday life is lost through urine, sweat, respiration, and faeces. Water lost must be replaced constantly. Drink one to two litres a day and increase this amount on your training days. Drinking only when thirsty is just filling up the tank when you are already empty. So constantly top up with eight or more glasses a day.

DIETARY FIBRE

This is found in grains (oats, oat bran, wheat, rye, soy, and linseeds) and in fruits and vegetables. An essential part of your nutrition, it helps absorb water and toxins, and it helps balance movement along the digestive tract, aiding in elimination of waste. It also increases the availability of vitamins and minerals.

VITAMINS AND MINERALS

All of the food groups mentioned provide a good balance of the vitamins and minerals vital to our bodily functions. Optimally, your vitamin and mineral needs will be met if produce is organic or homegrown. This reduces the sprays and chemicals put into your body, which cause added stress on your health. Taking supplements of good multivitamins and minerals is necessary if your intake of food groups is not enough, if you lead a busy life, or if you are a serious athlete.

CALLING THE SHOTS

Tactics are usually discussed before the game by the coach, trying to work out the opposition's weaknesses and develop a game plan to best exploit their deficiencies. Before each game, reinforce or tell your players what moves you want them to use today. Some coaches do not like to get too wrapped up with whom their team is playing against and would rather focus on their own side. Knowing and playing to your strengths is obviously necessary, but you must have the ability to change tactics if required. This is where your senior players and captain must take some control on the field and work towards developing a successful formula. Your moves or sequencing plays are trying to create an overlap or a mismatch in your favour. I use four players who have the ability to beat their opposition with strength or pace and try to give them room to exploit their advantage or mismatch. These players are called pressure points.

When John Hart coached the All Blacks, he would split each section of his team and name a senior player to oversee that part of the game. For example, ZinZan Brooke would be in charge of back row defence; Andrew Mertens, back line moves; Ian Jones, line-outs; Robin Brooke, receiving kickoffs; Frank Bunce, back line defence. This gave players extra responsibility on and off the field. Also, it gave them the opportunity to iron out any problems that may arise in their own departments, especially during a game where a coach cannot have much input. This concept is much like a business, where they have team leaders in place.

The captain has traditionally been a forward, with the intention of him leading from the front. This does not have to be the case as there have been many successful captains playing in the backs where they probably have a better vantage point and more time to assess the game. David Kirk (New Zealand), Nick Farr-Jones (Australia), and Will Carling (England) come to mind. In most teams, the number ten, known as the fly-half or first five-eight, does most of the calling of moves or plays. This player must be cool and confident in his decision-making. He must obviously be a good communicator and not be easily distracted. A lot of teams have too many moves, with some being too complicated. It is much better to have five or six back line moves with everyone knowing and performing them well. Only a couple of these should be high risk.

Each player should know when and from what phase they will receive the ball, but they should always be ready. Often a back row move or a crash in midfield may take place before the backs try their strike move. On most occasions, a try will not be scored from first phase, but it can be done. In every play, each player has a job. It could be to distribute, hit the line at pace, run good angles, or create a diversion off the ball. The caller of the moves needs to work out which is the best zone to attack at, with the likelihood of breaking the defence. Therefore, most of the right calls come from what the opposition is up to defensively. Is their fullback not wide enough to cover the wipers or long-raking kick? Is the blindside winger too flat and not helping the fullback to cover the box kick? Is the open side winger coming in to spot tackle and leaving the outside man unmarked? Is their defensive line spread out or standing close together? Are they playing man-on or a one-out drift defence?

SPRINT TRAINING

Sprint training should be a part of every serious rugby player's regime. How much you include should be determined on body type and playing position. You cannot be too fast. Flexibility, strength, and agility are the main areas of concern. Flexibility will give you a longer stride and a higher leg and arm action. Leg strength is necessary for pushing off the ground and pulling your leg back after your foot hits the ground. Upper-body strength is required for arm power and lung capacity. Agility helps combine flexibility with strength. During a rugby season, most players' aerobic fitness is good due to match fitness, but very often their speed or sharpness declines. A good coach should recognise this and incorporate sprint training into practice sessions. This will reactivate old and new fast twitch fibres, which will promote speed.

Pliometrics are a useful tool in sprint training. A rope ladder is an excellent way to help leg speed. Pliomtetrics is based around tricking the body into believing more muscle fibres are required in the areas that are used in running. It's similar to weight training. If you exaggerate your length or height of stride, for example, more muscle groups will form. Practice sessions that include running backwards, hopping on one leg or two, bounding for height, bounding for length, butt kicks, running sideways, and resistance training will achieve good results. It is essential to include plenty of stretching and flexibility training before and after pliometrics training. Otherwise, too much muscle alone will make you too tight, and you may break instead of bouncing in contact. Warming down and stretching after practices and games will help your elasticity immensely. Some players' running styles need improvement, even if new techniques feel uncomfortable to begin with. A lot of players do not have a desirable knee lift. A good knee lift can extend their stride and make them faster. Stand tall and strong with a slight lean forward. Relax your hands. Remember to keep your head and toes up. Below I have given examples of sprint sessions.

EXAMPLE 1

3 times 300 metres in 45 to 50 seconds. 3 times 200 metres in 30 to 33 seconds. 3 times 150 metres in early 20s. Then repeat once over each distance. Vary recovery time due to fitness level, but use a time of between 60 and 90 seconds as a guide.

EXAMPLE 2

10 sets of 50-metre sprints in 7 seconds with a 50-metre follow-through after each sprint. It takes around 23 seconds to jog through at a steady clip. Once again, vary your recovery time. A good guide is to start with 10 seconds of recovery after the first set, then increase it by 10 seconds after every set.

EXAMPLE 3

4 sets of 100 metres in 15 seconds per set, with 90, 60 and then 30 seconds recovery between each run.

EXAMPLE 4

6 sets of 300-metre runs with two and a half minutes of recovery time after each set.

EXAMPLE 5

10 sets of 60-metre runs in 10 seconds with 40 seconds recovery break. Then 10 sets of 30-metre runs in 5 seconds with 20 seconds of recovery time.

EXAMPLE 6

8 times 7-metre sprints, and walk back. 30-second rest after the 8 sprints. 6 times 15-metre sprints and walk back. 1-minute rest after the 6 sprints. 4 times 25-metre sprints and walk back. 2-minute rest after the 4 sprints. Repeat 2 or 3 times.

Remember: no pain, no gain. Happy training!

ROLE OF THE COACH

The coach has the role of communicator and teacher of skills.

A RUGBY COACH IS:
- a leader
- an innovator
- an organiser
- a hero
- a manager
- a fall guy
- a friend
- a decision maker
- a counselor
- a communicator
- a teacher
- a role model
- a motivator

THE COACH NEEDS TO HAVE:
- knowledge of the game
- practices that develop skill
- positive attitudes which help develop discipline

Remember: The key to the development of attitudes is enjoyment. The key to the development of enjoyment is variety.

COACHING CONTAINS THREE BASIC AREAS OF RESPONSIBILITY:
- player fitness
- skills and development
- motivation

THE BASIC REQUIREMENTS OF A COACH ARE:

- A sound knowledge of the game
- The ability to instill the right attitudes in players
- Effective planning and organisational skills
- The ability to detect problem areas and correct these quickly and effectively
- Flexibility with regard to resources available to him
- To act as a role model for the players under him
- Belief in his own ability so that he can motivate players to improve performance
- Ability to communicate with players as individuals
- Being prepared to keep up-to-date with current coaching methods
- The ability to generate team spirit by making all players feel like they're part of the team
- Evaluating team performance constantly and being able to analyse individual weaknesses and remedy them

CHECKLIST FOR COACHES

Use the suggestions below as a helpful guide from pre-season to the start of competition.

LIASON WITH PLAYERS

- Make initial contact, i.e., letters to individuals, verbal contact.
- Discuss pre-season fitness programme and outline main objectives.
- Introduce assistant coaches and managers, if appointed at this stage.
- Take particular care to make new players welcome.
- Ask committee members, e.g., the club captain, to talk briefly about the club, the organization, the amenities, etc.
- Plan pre-season sessions carefully. Make sure there is a balance between use of the ball and activities involving cardio-respiratory work, i.e., a five kilometre run.

LAISON WITH PARENTS

- Organise meeting to discuss team policy on washing jerseys, oranges for halftime, the medical kit, etc.
- Organise someone to be in charge of team funds, if necessary.
- Discuss parental support on sideline – this is to be positive at all times.
- Discuss your requirements with regard to dress, punctuality of players, loyalty, etc.

Liaison with Managers

- Outline their role within the team.
- Write down clear guidelines on their function.
- Stress the need to maintain discretion on all team matters.
- Offer them time to discuss relevant matters with the team during the season.

Liaison with Team at the Time the Squad Is Finalised

- Clearly state your objectives for the season to the team.
- Set achievable goals at various stages of the season.
- Stress discipline, punctuality, and team loyalty at all times, both on and off the field.
- Discuss the policy on team dress and demand high standards with regard to boots and gear.
- Appoint the captain and vice captain early on and stress the need for team cooperation with these people.

COACHING ETHICS

SENIOR TEAMS

- Be reasonable with players regarding your demands of time, energy, and enthusiasm. Remember they have other interests.
- Teach players to abide by the rules of the game.
- Try to give all players in the squad equal opportunity to develop.
- If a player needs to be disciplined or stood down, make sure you explain the reasons why to him personally, prior to team announcement.
- Lead by example, both on and off the field.
- Remember that variation in training is essential; a night off now and then does not do any harm.
- Follow the advice of a doctor in determining injuries when you are uncertain of the severity.
- Get input from players at training but reserve your own right as a coach to have the final say. Don't be afraid to use other personnel in training.
- Make sure that managers and other personnel with the team are aware of their roles early in the season.
- Be positive in your approach to training. Try to show appreciation for things done well rather than ridicule players for mistakes made.
- Explain early in the season the necessity for punctuality, discipline, and commitment at training.
- Discuss with players your policy on reserves.
- Set your standards high early in the season and make sure players have your respect at all times.
- Discuss your policy on dress and team gear with players and enforce this at all times.

- Never get drawn into discussing players with other players, spectators, or club personnel. Be very loyal to your team.

JUNIOR COACHING CODE

- Be reasonable in your demands on the young players' time, energy, and enthusiasm. Remember that they have other interests.
- Teach your players that the rules of the game are mutual agreements which no one should evade or break.
- Group players according to age, height, skill, and physical maturity whenever possible.
- Avoid overplaying the talented players. The "just average" players need and deserve equal time.
- Remember that children play for fun and enjoyment and that winning is only part of it.
- Ensure that equipment and facilities are appropriate to the age and ability of the players.
- The scheduling and length of practice times and games should take into consideration the maturity level of the children.
- Develop team respect for the ability of opponents, as well as for the judgement of referees and opposing coaches.
- Follow the advice of a doctor in determining when an injured player is ready to play again.
- Remember that children need a coach they can respect. Be generous with your praise when it is deserved and set a good example.
- Make a personal commitment to keep yourself informed on sound coaching principles and the principles of the growth and development of children.

PRACTICE PLANNING
AND ORGANISATION

This chapter includes some important things to keep in mind when planning your practices.

ORGANISATION

- Plan practice sessions considering:
  - Time of season
  - Who you are playing next and how you want to play them
  - Number of practices to prepare
  - What is needed and what should be worked on, which is partly determined by how the team did in the last game and what the team goals are
- Write down what you are going to do and follow it – within reason.
- Write down drills and the objectives of each.
- Consider how much time is needed for each drill.
- Consider player placement.

PRACTICE CONTENT

- This should be determined by:
  - Time of season
  - Points under "organisation" above
  - Number of players on the team
- Always include some conditioning work.
  - Amount depends on level of competition
  - Less as players become fitter

- Keep drills simple.
- Ensure maximum participation.
- Follow your practice plan.
- Avoid team talks during practice.
- Always include some basic development.

PLANNING THE PRACTICE

- Consider the length of the practice.
- List the number of areas you want to cover.
- List these areas in order of importance for that practice.
- Proportion total practice time in order of priority.
- Keep a chart of time per area.

WHICH DRILLS TO USE

- Use drills that really help develop the area you want to work on.
- Use simple drills that combine both skills and objectives.
- Use drills that keep everyone involved.
- Use drills that combine conditioning and basic development.
- Know the drill before using it.

GUIDELINES FOR
TRAINING SESSIONS

All aspects of training can be related to the four principles of team play. They are:
- Go forward
- Support the ball carrier
- Watch your continuity of attack
- Put pressure on the opposition

WARM-UP (10–15 MINUTES)

KEY POINTS
- Have adequate balls and cones available. If possible, have one ball for every two players.
- Use a variety of different grids.
- Involve players in stretching exercises during session.
- Demand discipline and concentration in all aspects of warm-up.

UNIT WORK (20–30 MINUTES)
BACKS AND FORWARDS APART

KEY POINTS
- Stress communication between players, e.g., forwards call for the ball in mauls, backs pass ball on and back up.
- Involve all members of the squad. Reserves can be used to assist in setting up situations on attack and defence.

48

- Work on skills relating to the previous Saturday's performance, with regard to improvements needed.

TEAM TRAINING (20–30 MINUTES)

KEY POINTS
- Look to both attack and defence.
- Divide field up and look at team strategy in relation to each area.
- Keep discussion to a minium at this stage of training.
- Relate training to actual game situation.
- Stress team discipline and communication.
- Build the confidence of individuals on your team.

COOL-DOWN (5 MINUTES)

KEY POINTS
- Simply quiet down activity at the end of training.
- Leave players with positive thoughts about next Saturday's game.

The Importance of Grid Work in Team Training

Grid work provides many benefits, such as:
- Enabling a whole range of skills to be practiced in a confined space
- Developing understanding between players in situations closely related to the game
- Sharpening players reactions with regards to acceleration, swerving, sidestepping, passing, etc.
- Making players aware of the need to communicate
- Giving players practice at taking the right options and making quick decisions
- Developing special awareness and teaching players to be switched on in any situation
- Developing fitness while sharpening ball skills
- Developing the use of peripheral vision

The Use of Grids

- Use grids for a purpose, i.e., skill development, warm-up, fitness.
- Try to base the skills being emphasised on the strength and weaknesses of your game. Look at areas of concern from the previous Saturday.
- Try to invent your own grids to overcome a particular lack of skill in the team. Encourage individuals during grid work. Be positive with players.
- Make sure grids used are applicable to the age group of your team.
- Demand that grid work is of a high standard, and insist on a high level of skill and concentration.

ORGANISATION AND SAFETY

- Maintain lines during activities.
- Stress the use of correct skills at all times.
- Stress the use of safe body position in picking up the ball and catching high balls in grid work.
- Players must avoid contact unless a contact skill is being developed.
- If a skill is not being done correctly, stop the grid and explain the need for more concentration.

Team Managers' Duties

Your team manager can be a person of considerable importance to you. He can take off your shoulders many of the details necessary in successfully running your team.

It is suggested that, after study, you discuss the appended list of duties with him to reach a working arrangement that will ensure a successful, efficient, and happy team — and coach.

Pre-Season

- Assist the coach in contacting all of the previous year's team to find out if they are available for the coming season. This should be done at least a fortnight before the first training run is scheduled.
- Ensure that all players in your team squad have completed the annual registration form and that it has been handed to the secretary of the club captain.
- Check the players' eligibility to play for your team. Has the necessary transfer from another club been approved? Is the player within the prescribed age or weight (where applicable) for the grade? Are reinstatements from League required, or is regrading required?

During the Season

- The manager is responsible for making sure that the players' current addresses and telephone numbers are up to date. The secretary is to be informed of any changes of address.

- Collect players' subscriptions and pay in to the secretary or the treasurer.
- Keep a supply of team sheets and replenish them from the club captain when necessary.
- First-aid kits are the responsibility of the manager and must be kept fully stocked.
- Make sure the practice balls are available and pumped up properly.
- Attend all practices with the coach and make such arrangements as he requires on team matters.
- Advise the coach of all players who miss training and if reasons for their absence are not known, get in touch with them to ascertain the cause.
- Attend coaching and other meetings when the coach is unable to attend.
- Make sure that all your team's players are informed of all club functions, social and otherwise, team or club.
- Be responsible for team funds and savings. Write everything down, get receipts for all monies paid out, and ensure that the team money is lodged in a special team fund account, *not* in the manager's own bank account. The coach is to make adequate secure arrangements for the working of the account (two signatures, etc.).
- Organise visits to hospitalised players.
- Ensure that proper application is made through the club and in sufficient time for the approval of the rugby union to be obtained for your team to travel on any trip arranged.
- Organise transport to outside grounds when necessary.
- Ensure that the team's emergency gear, such as shorts, jerseys, socks, laces, garters, hammers and pliers for boots, are readily available on Saturday.
- Ensure that the water bottles and first-aid kit are available and that the bottles are full of fresh water.

- Ensure that a ball is available and is the right pressure.
- Ensure that a team sheet is available and is made out under the coach's direction.
- Collect the players' valuables and place them in a bag before the game and do not lose control of it until belongings have been returned to their owners. If the security container in the dressing room is used or the dressing room door is locked, retain custody of the keys until the game is finished. Do not forget that injured players may need to get in.
- Collect players' laundry fees.
- Make sure that all players are neatly attired in clean jerseys, shorts, and sox, and that boots have been cleaned. Advise coach of any deficiencies in players' gear.

AFTER GAME

- See that any injured players, if not being taken to hospital, have transport and someone to see that they get home or back to the club safely.
- Ensure that all jerseys, shorts, sox, etc., are accounted for and are in the proper bags (gear manager?).
- Check the dressing room when all are finished to ensure that no clothing, towels, bottles, etc., have been left.
- Ensure that the keys of the dressing room and security lockers are returned to the club house.
- After the game, phone the results to the secretary. All that is required is the grade and the result (points).
- See that the result of the game is phoned back to the club—unless you are coming straight back to the club.

- See that the secretary gets a team report from your coach.
- Ensure that the necessary injury reports are made out and forwarded to the secretary or the insurance officer.

After the Season

- Check on the availability of coach, manager, and players for the next season—at least two games before the end of the season.
- Ensure that the coach completes a report on your team for the season for inclusion in the club's annual report, and make sure that the secretary gets it.
- Maintain contact with the team members during the off season, at socials, sporting activities, etc., with the object of keeping them fit and a "family."

Club Manual

- Managers are strongly advised to check with club as to the whereabouts of the club manual and read parts that are relevant to their job.
- Note: Any player ordered off by the referee must attend the next meeting of the judicial committee of the union.

What a Coach Wants from Backs

General

- Good communication
- Ability to win a man-on-man competition
- Ability to use one's feet and change pace quickly
- Ability to create space for others
- Quickness (not necessarily speed)
- Ability to rapidly read a situation
- Equal ability to pass with both hands
- Sound defence
- Ability to kick punts, chip, grubber
- Being proactive

Fullbacks

- Ability to be a strike player by entering the line
- Ability to change the angle of running when entering a line
- Ability to take high balls
- Good positional play
- Ability to see himself as the joker in the pack and to pop up everywhere
- Ability to work with his wings to become a formidable force
- To come into the line as a decoy
- To come in to give an overlap
- To be strong in the tackle
- To have a good boot

WINGS

Wings should be like fullbacks and able to do everything a good fullback can do, so read what I have said about fullbacks.

- See when the game is going into touch and come inside.
- Form with other wing and fullback a counterattacking team.
- Sound defence.
- Realise how difficult he is to mark if he moves all over the field like a number eight, especially when he is the blindside wing with his side attacking.
- Vary running lines and point of attack.
- Pace helps—it's a gift of God—but also have the ability to link and not necessarily go to ground.
- Keep the ball in the field of play, so as not to give opponents line-outs.
- When you see a player heading across the field, give him the angle by coming inside to take a scissors.

CENTRES

Everything I said under "General" applies particularly to centres. I believe their jobs to be the most difficult in the game.

- Create for another some space, a gap, an overlap. "I create for my wing—a golden ball."
- The ability to slow a game down and quicken it up.
- The ability to change pace.
- Always committing an opponent or beating him. He won't always do this by running across the field, but even that can work if his partner then comes through close and straight.
- Play off and with another as a pair.
- Communicate in attack and defence.

- Defend, especially in an opponent's face.
- Be the first into a tackled ball to retrieve it from your partner who is tackled.
- Primary and secondary support.
- *Work off the ball* is almost more important than *work with the ball.*
- Dominate his opponent.
- Play both inside and outside and do not be a basher.
- Communicate with the touch judge and indicate to his fellows the offside line. Communication.

FLY-HALVES

- To get his backs away.
- To determine the most effective backline alignment in defence and attack. He must vary his attacking alignment according to the situation.
- Be in calm control.
- He is a key support runner and cannot except this from his game.
- Defence must be strong.
- Vary his personal game. Certainly he must as much as possible commit his opponent as well as the loose forwards and not allow them to slide across in defence without first checking them.
- Have a competent boot.
- If his outside players are limited for space, it is most likely his fault. He is responsible for the good play of those outside him.
- He must have the ability, like a centre, to crack a line.
- Like the inside centre, he must be a playmaker and not a basher.
- He must attack and be positive.
- Vary your depth.

SCRUM-HALVES

- Give a good, clean, quick, and accurate service to his outside man.
- Be a force on attack around the edges.
- Be a good support player by always being an metre inside and slightly behind the man with the ball. A big ask.
- Be able to vary his play by using the boot, but, like the flyhalf, rarely and with effect. Form with the back row a formidable attacking quartet.
- Be a pain in defence by exerting pressure.
- He must direct his forwards in rucks and mauls, pulling out and pushing in. He has the same function in defence from rucks and mauls, especially near the line.
- He must liaise between backs and forwards.
- Forwards get tired and don't think. He can play a big role here as encourager and instructor.

Scrums,
by Basil Bey

Scrumming
Part One

It is usual, in the front row, for the hooker to bind over the shoulders of his two props and grip the prop under his outside armpit. Some hookers prefer to loosen their right shoulder to give them more stretch on their own ball, but with the put-ins nowadays that seems hardly necessary and the bind that is equally tight on both sides is a very strong one.

The loosehead prop will bind on his opponent's back from underneath the opposing tighthead's arm. The higher his bind on the back, the stronger and more stable he will feel, although props all have their own theories and explanations, such as the short arm grip and so on.

The tighthead will do the same except that he will bind above the arm of his opposing loosehead and onto his back.

Locks bind on one another; the taller, heavier lock is usually on the right-hand side to counter the natural wheel, and he normally will bind over the shoulder of the left-hand lock and down under his armpit. Some people feel that the lower the bind from the armpit, the tighter it is. Good point. The reason the tighthead's shoulder is over that of the loosehead lock (left lock) is that his shoulder will protrude and thus push the right hip of the hooker towards the scrum mouth, for the ball comes in on the left-hand side of the scrum. Outer arms of both locks go between the legs of the props and, ideally, round the leg and up on to the pocket of the prop. Some prefer to bind straight upwards, and some props will leave the jersey out to assist the lock to get a good grip. I prefer the pocket bind because being tighter, it actually pulls the props in towards the hooker.

Both flanks bind with their inside arms around the back of closest lock. It must be a tight bind initially so that as the props get down to scrum, the flanks steady them and give them a push in. Once down, both might like to loosen the bind somewhat to enable them to manoeuvre better in defence or attack or to flare out a bit from the scrum for various reasons, from obstructing the opposing scrum-half (on the lefthand side) to keeping the prop's hips square to the scrum.

The number eight, head between the two locks' buttocks, binds around the outside of their hips. Between the legs limits the freedom of the number eight.

SCRUMMING
PART TWO

A very important component of scrumming is the foot and body positions of the players. The law states that props must have shoulders above hips— a tough one when an opponent is pulling you down and you have to rely on a ref who played fullback all his life!

Backs should be parallel to the ground for obvious reasons—if your back is pointing to the sky, you will scrum towards the sky just as, if a scrum-half in delivering the ball to his flyhalf does not keep his back parallel to the ground, the ball that he passes will go, accordingly, awry. If your back is aiming at the sky, you do not get as much forward movement as you would if it were parallel to the ground although, as a prop, you might pop your opposite prop (something I always admired in rugby—I'm sorry it has been outlawed!).

Spines, unless you want to wheel, must be parallel to one another's so that we are all moving in the same direction and not pushing counter to one another.

61

Scrumming is very logical. Lean against a fence or a desk and put both hands on it. Then move your left foot forward and see where your hips and back go—you will find you are pushing to the right. Sometimes a hooker might complain that he has too much pressure on his left or right side from his lock and this twists his body the way he does not want it. Think carefully and move the lock's feet accordingly, to take the pressure off or put it on where you require it. Think about wheeling a scrum and see how this simple play can be used effectively.

Ideally, without a wheel or without trying to prevent a wheel, everyone should scrum with feet about at shoulder width, or a little more if you have narrow shoulders, apart and with feet equidistantly back to allow the backs to be parallel to the ground and to the touchline, with shoulders to the tryline. Props' feet will be a little closer to their shoulders, though spread apart as described, but if they are too much under their shoulders, their hips will be lifted by their locks and there will be no power. Locks and props (loose forwards pack down in much the same position as locks) must bend their knees or else they will plunge into the ground; locks will slide up and chaos will ensue. When locking a scrum, locks often like to straighten their knees and dig their feet into the ground. Think of pushing a stick into the ground. It is straight; therefore, the harder you push, the deeper it digs.

Flanks must get down with their props and with the same force as the locks.

Some coaches like their flanks to pack with their inside foot behind the outside foot so that the first stride will take them out to defend rather than pulling them in to the scrum. Coaches also talk about backs aligning their feet in similar fashion so that the first pace will pull them in or out as is desired—usually the foot closest to the touchline in front so that the first pace straightens up the player.

Most props like to have the outside foot just a little in front of the inside—it does support the body somewhat, although you lose a bit of pushing power. Your bum and thigh muscles are the biggest and you want to have them working at top strength.

Feet too far back for any player in the scrum make for lack of shoving power, too far forward make for bent back and downward pushing.

The bind is very important, but no more so than the foot positions of the players. There are all sorts of sophistications, such as one-half of the scrum, let us say the left, all having the left foot slightly behind the right, and vice versa, and then all players move in unison. When the ball goes in, you should flex your muscles as a group to become stronger and tighter.

No player in the scrum should lift his foot more than an inch off the ground for he and his scrum will be thrown backwards. A scrum advances in small steps: shuffle, shuffle, shuffle.

If a scrum goes up or down or even sideways, look at foot positions. If it disintegrates, especially bursting outwards, it is mostly the bind—a good bind makes up for all sorts of sins.

SCRUMMING
PART THREE: GETTING DOWN

The referees have taken much bite out of the way players like to get down to scrums. They also get in the way of the scrum-half so a quick put in, sometimes highly desirable, becomes almost impossible. Then, too, we have the *crouch, touch, engage* routine for schoolboys and something a little more truncated for the seniors; thus, there is less room between front rows and less power on the "hit."

There are so many theories of how to get down. Senior players normally work out what is most effective themselves through practising together against a machine and then opponents.

Two much used methods are:

METHOD ONE

Locks get in and flanks must get down with the props — it helps the props considerably. The front row crouches as though sitting on a lavatory seat, hips below shoulders. Feet should all be in the correct position.

The hooker is the captain of the tight scrum, and he must talk his players into scrumming readiness, so that on the ref's "engage," they are in a good position to come in, well bound, feet in the correct position, and with the hit on the correct shoulder. On your ball, for example, you possibly want to stop the opponents wheeling you forward on the loosehead (left side) in order to win a re-scrum, their ball. So the front row would come down with the tighthead leading and perhaps ahead of his hooker and loosehead prop.

Number eight normally looks about to see what is cooking and comes in just before the hit.

METHOD TWO

Same as above, the locks come in with flanks. Props put their feet back and put all their weight on their shoulders, as it were, whereas in the first method their weight is above their feet.

The hooker is important here. He has both feet forward and is leaning back, holding back his props whose weight and angles of inclination are pulling them into the scrum. The hooker here is in the position of the last man in a tug-of-war team.

His legs are bent and wide to give him the strength to hold his props, and indeed the other forwards, back. Then, as the ref gives the "engage," the hooker allows the props to fall into the scrum, coming down with them, and adjusting his feet to the most advantageous hooking position for him. The others, as in method one (above), should have their feet in the right position from the start.

This is a very powerful "get-down" that I should not recommend for young learns at schoolboy level.

The way the front row goes down decides upon the efficacy of your scrum on either ball.

A psychological advantage can be gained by the forwards who arrive first to the scrum and get organised quickly. Even if you are tired, your keenness to get on with the job can be depressing to the opposition. Former Ulster hooker Michael Pattern told me that scrumming is 50% technique and 50% concentration, so be focused at every scrum.

Line-outs,
by Basil Bey

Short Line-outs and Lifting

I suppose the easiest is a three-man. The three can move as a group up and down the line-out, and as they change direction, the opponents will always be a little late in following, which means there is an advantage. You could start with the three on the fifteen-metre mark. If the opponents do not follow suit, it is an easy line-out. If they do, you can move forward and then back again, or forward and forward. Here you have obviously two supporters and a jumper. The other thing you can do here is to have your jumper standing at the back of the three, but then just before the ball comes in, he can move late into the middle jumping position, thus getting a running start for his jump, enabling him to get a higher jump and therefore better support.

For another three-man, put two in the line-out and the jumper at scrum-half. The two in the line-out can move up and down, and then the scrum-half can move suddenly into the line-out as the thrower launches the ball. The hooker now becomes the scrum-half. That is even more effective as a four-man line-out, with three in the line and an extra jumper outside it. Again he comes into the jump at the last second.

I prefer four-man line-outs because you can use them rather like a concertina: two moving forward, two back. The second from the back moves in to support the second from the front or vice versa. You can start off with two at the back and two forward instead of moving (let me number them from the front: four, three, two, one) the hooker.

Two moves in to three to support, so four and two are supporting three. Vice versa, three moves to two. As they get better at this, you can start them moving. Imagine now if you put a jumper at scrum-half who comes in late anywhere amongst the four—this is almost impossible to counter. Then the hooker once more becomes the scrum-half.

I have also found that even from a full line-out that if you walk, let us say, your number eight up the side of the line-out just before the ball comes in and then if he suddenly moves into the gap between your first two men in the line-out, he will take everyone by surprise. He moves into the jump from about half a metre back from the gap, into which he moves so suddenly there is an extra unexpected man. As long as he is in the line-out before the ball leaves the hooker's hands, he is fine.

I like the hooker to throw after the jumper attains his height, but you will find that most jumpers have their own preferences and if it works, leave it. You see, if the opponents cannot read your line-outs, they do not know where the ball is going and they cannot arrange for their opposing jumper to be lifted into the right position. So what does it matter if my hooker waits for my jumper to attain full height? There will be no one up there with him, so accuracy of throw is more important than timing. This timing varies so much that I do not know what to say.

Certainly, the shorter ball should be put in hard and straight at the jumper's hands as he reaches full stretch. You can only stand on the side and call what you see— harder, slower, quicker—and tell the lock not to be kind to his hooker, but rather to insist on the throw being as he likes it. As for deep throws, most people prefer a lobbed ball coming down to the hands; therefore, the throw comes a little earlier, but to be honest, with a good lift, even the timing does not matter too much as long as the jump is where the opponents do not expect it.

Yes, more and more players do tape their thighs, and I do not discourage it, but nor do I insist on it. Why not tape your best jumper one practice and find out if he feels it makes a difference? I would say it does if your jumper, on his own jump, can get high enough for his support to come in on his thighs with their fingers pointing up the thighs. If your jumper does not get high on his own unassisted jump, it is extremely difficult to support the thighs because you have to bend down so low in getting your hands onto the thighs (or even shorts) that you will struggle to come out of the body angle you, as a supporter, have put yourself into. I should insist on a push, as opposed to a lift, in support. That is hands down, facing the ground and pushing up, rather than hands up and pulling. You then get a greater height because you are now getting your shoulders into the push, as well as your thighs, hips, and back. Ask you players to grab a barbell, hands underneath the bar and to raise it above their heads full stretch. Few will manage. But do it with your hands on the top of the bar and few will have any problem. That is the answer. The initial spring of the jumper helps enormously, for he should get high enough through his own lift so that your supporters' arms are already straightening.

LINE-OUTS

Particularly at school level you find opponents lifting early at two and four on your ball, and it is most disconcerting to the thrower and your jumper. Most referees do not blow this up, yet they should. That is why I believe in such variation in line-out techniques, even to the scrum-half appearing in the line-out with the jumper standing in the scrum-half position. At a signal the scrum-half moves out and the jumper moves in anywhere he wishes to jump and take the ball.

A variation that has died out to a large extent is the throw over the number eight's head, either to a back or to the number eight. If the ball is going to travel beyond the fifteen-metre mark, number eight can go beyond it once the ball leaves the thrower's hands, and the back can move within ten metres of the line-out. It is also effective from a short line-out, but good opponents will sometimes put their scrum-half near the fifteen-metre mark to smother. From a short line-out it is quick and catches the opponents more often than not. The unexpected so often succeeds spectacularly in rugby.

We often hear the cry from spectators: "But why do they not contest the line-outs?" when referring to the side not throwing the ball in. Many non-throwing sides will contest anywhere outside their own twenty-two, and some jumpers are expert at anticipating and spoiling—hence the emphasis on movement and variation in a line-out by the side throwing in.

Why do some teams not contest a line-out in their own twenty-two, or sometimes not at all? Well, take a side like the English who are so expert at setting up a rolling maul or a drive from a line-out: if there's enough to have two people lifting the one who is trying to capture, let us say, the English ball, then you are going to have only four defenders fighting that maul. The others are out of action at a particularly crucial time, for the defence one is allowed to offer to that maul is opposing pressure only: you may not bring it to the ground.

A good general rule in defending the rolling maul is to take the maul into touch; begin your push early from behind the jumper to the touchline. It is particularly effective if the ball is thrown to two, but it can work even on a four ball. At least you are cutting down on the blindside (although I must admit this can backfire in the case of the four ball). Good sides will set up their mauls from deeper throws—four, five, or six even. They are hell to stop close to the line, and the temptation is always there to pull them down. This is one place where the law should be changed in favour of the defender, for if the ball is moved to the rear of a maul, what chance have you of getting to it and wresting it away or spoiling it? None! (Refer to the "Maul Defence" chapter for some other options.)

There is less emphasis nowadays on getting in front of your opposing jumper and turning your back to him in the jump, especially at two, but it is still effective at times.

On my own line-out, I always pull out a loose forward and put him at flyhalf and then move everyone across in defence, thus establishing out-defence or what some people call shift-defence. Thus you can deal with a fullback coming into the line-in attack. I feel that the flanker has a small defensive part to play from his normal position in the line-out. Some will disagree with me. In defence, most will put number eight on to the flyhalf; other loose forwards, depending upon the situation (as with eight, in fact), will defend the peel round the back or come up slightly behind and just inside (closer to touchline) the number eight and thus cover anyone slipping in from blindside wing and so on.

On the opponents' line-out ball on my line, my blindside wing will take the flyhalf position and the flyhalf will drop back to take the pass from scrum-half in the unlikely event of our taking their ball. He can quickly adjust from there and still come into the defence setup should the opponents move the ball along the backs or drive round front or back. Some prefer to leave him where he should be and bring in the blindside wing to the defence lineup anyway, leaving all three loose forwards in the line-out to defend the maul or ruck, and this is, considering the effectiveness of the modern line-out, probably the best anywhere near your own line.

At all times the hooker should guard, with his life, his blindside and should endeavour not to be sucked in to the maelstrom of maul or ruck. At times, of course, he will not be able to avoid being dragged in.

GRASS ROOTS RUGBY

In the beginning children play rugby because their mates do and because they are encouraged to do so by proud parents. Coaching at this stage is normally performed admirably by one or two keen fathers. Being part of a team environment is a very positive way to develop social skills for kids of all ages. It is great that a position in a rugby team can accommodate any body type. There is a place for everyone! At any level, a successful team must have a balance of stars and workers to complement each other. The only truly global game of soccer has become more popular worldwide, as parents consider it a safer game for their children to play, but rugby is growing in many countries.

School-boy rugby is some of the best rugby you can play. The passion and support you can get from representing your school and its history is hard to reproduce in the years to follow. In some countries such as Canada and the United States, rugby starts at the secondary school level. A lot of teachers take on coaching with good results, mostly due to their people management and communication skills.

A lot of young players are giving up rugby in New Zealand because they have increasing work and family commitments. Also, a lot of young people are choosing the adventure of travelling overseas to work and experience life. Others continue to play rugby for many good reasons, such as health and fitness, team comraderie, or maybe to earn respect in their community.

"SO, WHERE TO FROM HERE?"
ACADEMY STYLE VERSUS THE CLUB SCENE.

Opinions are varied with many people wanting to emphasise the importance of club rugby. It is great when the players who have made the big time come back to club rugby to share knowledge and experiences with clubmates. This raises the standard of teammates' and oppositions' play, trying to aspire them to greater heights. Club rugby is the heart and soul of this great game. It is difficult to interfere with the enjoyment of the club culture and to separate and develop a player with special talent in the pursuit of excellence. The problem is that ninety-five percent of clubs don't have representative players to call on to share their wealth of knowledge. Therefore, young talent will probably never get top-quality coaching unless these players are identified early and given special attention. Most club sides are coached by a former player of the same club with good intentions, but it can be a difficult job with limited resources. To insure success in the future, promising players should have the opportunity to be the best they can be. It is a tragedy that so many players never reach their full potential.

In 1976, the Australian Olympic team that went to Montreal returned home with no gold medals. How things have changed. Why? The Australian Institute of Sport was introduced in 1977 to enable the talented athletes of Australia to train, study, and excel at their respective sports. No stone was left unturned. Coaches, doctors, sports psychologists, chiropractors, dieticians, business and media experts, all with a common goal, were consulted. A nation prepared to go that extra yard for success. An interesting example of this was their seating arrangements at the third test versus the 2001 Lions in Sydney. To counteract 20, 000 British and Irish supporters, Australian stadium officials, in their wisdom, put the Lions fans in the highest seats, at the end of the ground in darkness. The local fans were placed along the sides of the field under bright lights. They were given yellow hats to wear. On the field, players would have felt surrounded by Australian fans.

The Lions concept of only playing every four years creates a huge following when they do tour.

72

It is great that four nations, usually at each other's throats (especially the English and Irish), can come together to support a rugby union side. The continued debate over the strength of the northern and southern hemispheres' games also adds to the enormous interest.

MODERN RUGBY

The professional era has brought rugby-playing nations closer together. They play each other more often, which gives them more opportunity to learn from each other, and playing at a higher level promotes better play. The strength and standard of coaching has also improved around the world, so no side has a huge edge over another in this department. A lot of good coaching advice is now available on the internet, and many experienced coaches are working in other countries and sharing their knowledge. Many New Zealand players are also playing overseas because they cannot earn the same money in New Zealand. This obviously weakens club rugby in New Zealand and rugby at the national level, but it is difficult to compete with the British pound or the Japanese yen. I think New Zealand has enough depth to handle it, and this gives more opportunities to good young players. Rugby is the national sport in New Zealand, and the All Blacks will always be in the top bracket of teams. However, I do not think they will ever dominate as in the past and win game after game after game. That is not good for sport anyway, and the top six countries can now beat one another on any given day. The top players in each country are training in similar ways and getting good coaching. That is the professional era.

The skills of Japanese rugby players are very good. The huge advantage New Zealand players have is they are bought up as children in a rugby environment, so they can learn the game from a young age through watching the national sport or by playing themselves. This can develop rugby experience from a young age. It's important to know situations on the field and how to be proactive in reading the game. Rugby is a lot about taking the right options and making correct decisions. Good tactics often come from what the defence is doing, having the ability to read this, and knowing what is the best form of attack.

FLAIR VERSUS STRUCTURE

Flair is too often coached out of rugby players to fit into the game plan or the so-called structure of the team. Each player should be coached as an individual. We are not coaching rugby so much as we are coaching Johnny. The coach is not bigger than the game or the development of human beings expressing themselves on the field. Do not sacrifice this for a "win at all cost" attitude as this will scare players away from the game. Rugby should be enjoyed by all, both during and after the game. I know you cannot look at life through rose-tinted glasses either, but look to inspire. If the plays are too high-risk, and too many mistakes are being made, then the player concerned should be aware and be responsible for his actions.

Welcome to coaching. It is a fine line. One good coach told me once, "If it feels right, then go with it." But you are still accountable for your mistakes. It would be a sad day when individuality or playing off the cuff was not encouraged. Look at the left side of the brain versus the right side: left side for logic, right side for reactor. Sometimes our obsession with analysis and organization smothers talent rather than releasing it, and tenses up rather than relaxing. We inhibit the game when we restrict genius in our attempts to win. Do not stifle talent. Have the courage to be above that.

SPORTS PSYCHOLOGY

Sports psychology is nothing new and nothing to be afraid of. It is just that a lot of people are starting to realise its importance. Over the years we have all heard many clichés, such as, "Defence is all in the head," "Top two inches," and "It is who wants it the most," etc. All of these are correct, but few coaches tell you how you should be thinking. How do I remain confident, motivated, determined, focused, etc.? Hopefully we can help you in that department. Sports psychology focuses on every thought you have that relates to your sport. How you feel driving to training. Your pep-talk at halftime. How you feel the day after a game, etc. So it is nothing new and nothing to be afraid of. The overriding factor and what we are all aiming for is believing in yourself. The four main topics that all lead towards believing in yourself are motivation, confidence, anxiety control, and focusing.

MOTIVATION

There are two types of motivation: intrinsic and extrinsic. Extrinsic or external motivation comes from outside influences, such as a rep coach is coming to watch you play today, a friend or family member is coming to watch you play today, or pressure on your team position by a teammate. You may be marking a high-profile player this week, and you want to have a big game against him or her. Or perhaps a local derby. All motivation is good, so use what you can when you can. It is all good and all positive.

Intrinsic or internal motivation comes from within. You are your own critic, and you must be completely honest with yourself, striving for a complete performance and wanting to be the best you can be. You know how well you have played after the game, and you do not need people to tell you. Sometimes people will tell you that you played well when you know you did not, and other times you will be criticized unjustly. You are the best jugde, if you remain honest. If you can get a good intrinsic or internal motivation system going, then it can be there for you every week, as opposed to extrinsic, which is not. Former Canterbury captain Don Hayes would look himself in the mirror before he went out to play and ask himself if he was going to have a big game today. Contrast the warm sensation you get walking off the field with your head held high to that empty, gutted feelling you get after playing below your ability when you may have lost.

CONFIDENCE

Confidence is an emotion and a thought pattern. Like any other emotion, it can be turned on and off with practice. Actors have to learn to show different emotions when required, such as pain, sadness, laughter, and joy, just to name a few. They can turn emotions on and off like the flick of a switch. Confidence can be turned on by self-talk and even without references. You need confidence to be successful at any sport, and it's necessary for some more than others. I spoke to former Canterbury cricketer and now coach about this, and he said you have to be totally positive when you come out to bat, even if your average score is not so high. You must walk out as if you own the park. He also said good players can rise to pressure situations. I guess that is the case in all sports and sometimes in life, when you have to stand up and be counted.

Remember: confidence = success = pleasure.

It sure worked for Mohammed Ali.

Negative thoughts are a wasted emotion. Don't have negative thoughts on match day. Do your analyzing the next day or at the next training. Some people get themselves down for various reasons, such as work or family problems, relationship problems, bad whether, or a bad referee decision. Mistakes made by themselves or by teammates can be a big issue. So how do we push anxiety away when these problems arise? Self-talk. Focus on the solution rather than the problem. If you have problems at home, try to leave them there and use your sport as a chance to clear your mind and regroup. If the weather is not so good, think to yourself that any day is a good day to play this great game with your mates. Any day is a good day to wear the jersey. As for referees' decisions, I know it is hard sometimes, but try and work-with them. You cannot beat them. Penalties will kill any team. I would sometimes expect a referee to make four bad decisions during a game so when he made one I would not let it get me down. I would think, *Well, there is one out of the way.* If you expect it, then it is not a big deal.

The last and most common anxiety issue is how to deal with mistakes or failure. First, if a teammate is not doing so well, then the onus is on his or her teammates to keep his or her confidence up. Do not be harsh or criticize too much as it will do no one any good. Give him or her a lift or a pat on the back instead. Stay positive. The same goes if it is you who has made the mistake. Stay calm and push that play back in your memory bank and focus on the next play. A trick I would often use if I made one or two mistakes early in a game was to think to myself, *I am too much of a good player to let one or two mistakes ruin my whole game or my whole day. I have too much to offer to let that happen.* That was enough to keep my confidence up and make me able to focus on the next play.

FOCUSING

Focusing is the ability to put everything together and put it into practice. You must be able to use everything you have learned over the years. You must be able to use all your experience on match day. Apply yourself to produce good results. Do not leave it on the training paddock or in the dressing shed. It does not matter how confident, motivated, fast, skilled, honest, or strong you are if you can not put it all together and do the business. Focus on the moment. Playing rugby is made up of hundreds of decisions. It all comes down to option-taking. Focus on each moment that presents itself to you, and try to do the best you can. Sometimes you do not have to think because you instinctively make the correct decision. Your subconscious takes over because you have perfomed the required skill many times in previous games or at training, because you have experience.

Some people have trouble blocking out interferences. It is especially important for goal kickers to do this so they can produce their best kick. Try to first clear your mind. Some people like to do this by thinking of something outside of rugby, like surfing or eating chocolate. This may clear their mind and defuse the pressure of the situation. Then refocus on the technique of kicking the goal or perhaps making a good line-out throw. Goal kickers need to be relaxed, whereas some players play better when they are a little pumped up. This helps them focus better and apply themselves. Others get nervous, and the pressure affects their confidence and their game. So you need to know what works best for you. What is pressure? It is only other people's expectations.

Real-life stories are good motivation sometimes, especially when things are not going so great. One story I like is about a twenty-two-year-old man in America who had no family, no friends, and a dead-end job. All he had was a decent girlfriend who eventually dumped him. He decided to kill himself, but at the last moment he realised that he needed help and booked himself into a mental hospital. His name is Billy Joel.

When you feel physically exhausted, it is a scientific fact that you have twenty percent of your energy left. Animals in the wild have been recorded doing unbelievable feats when they were being chased and were running for their lives. Also, soldiers in the Vietnam War say they ran for miles through the jungle when running because of fear. Most rugby players never get into that twenty-percent zone, but some can and do. So next time you are very tired but need to defend your line for another five minutes, look for it. It is there.

THE RUCK

Preparing for contact is most important, The basic continuity section later deals with proper technique. A half-turn by your upper body as you take your power step will help you turn the right way in the tackle. Remember, body before the ball. Look to run at holes or at least at an outside shoulder, hoping to break the line. This also enhances your chances of unloading in the tackle. Fight to stay on your feet so your support has time to get there and to make more ground. Some teams like to go straight to ground on the last phase before giving the ball to the backs, since fast ruck ball is best for the backs to run off (e.g., A. C. T. Brumbies). If you feel in danger of being held up, then you also must go to ground. Try to fall inwards towards your support. This also makes the scrum-half's job easier when he/she tries to clear the ball after the cleanout.

Also, try to place the ball at a full arm's length. The first support players should clean out the opposition players who are within one metre of the ball and who are an obvious threat. When blowing over or cleaning out the ruck, try to hit on the up and stay on your feet. This will keep you in the game and not flopping over. The referee will also be happy. I realise that sometimes it is difficult to keep your feet. Sometimes you will have to roll players from both sides out of the way to free up the ball. I think the last support player at ruck time should stand over and protect the ball with one leg on top of the ball so the ruck is not over and the opposition can not come around and interfere with your scrum-half or halfback. The pick and go is always an option by any of the support players to continue momentum.

THE MAUL

The line-out is a good starting point to set a steady base for a good driving maul because you can often get your blocks in quickly. It is also possible to do this when receiving a kickoff. To initiate a maul from broken play, it is sometimes difficult to stay on your feet long enough to enable your support or blocks to arrive. It can be done by making a conscious decision to pull up short of the opposition, standing in a strong position with a fend. Hopefully, you can stay on your feet. Your support will come from the inside, so you need someone to quickly position themselves as an outside block to keep the opposition away and set a good platform. The ball must then be moved and stay at the back of the maul where it is safe and available for the scrum-half/halfback when required.

Continue to keep a low body position to help you push. Maintain stability by binding. Drive from your legs and keep a straight back. The driving maul is a good way to make the opposition commit and not stand off waiting for the runners or the backs. I think it is best for two or three players to break off the back of the maul to set up a good, quick, go-forward ball for the backs, instead of giving them a static ball from a maul which has stopped. The best use of a maul is to get over the opposition's line to score. Patience and good communication are required. Everyone needs to know how far away the tryline is and they need to make sure the maul stays intact long enough to complete the movment.

MAUL DEFENCE

The maul has always been an effective way to make ground and gain forward momentum. It is probably the most effective scoring weapon and is the only way you can use many players to protect the ball. Therefore, it is important to have a strategy to counteract a strong mauling side. Most mauls start from a line-out or kickoff return. Some teams also have the ability to set a maul from a ruck or general play. At line-out time, it is natural for defensive players to quickly assemble to counteract the drive from the attacking side. In doing this, a line-out has quickly become a maul. If the defence only sends one player into contact, it is regarded as a tackle situation; therefore, the defender is within his rights to try and push or pull the ball carrier to the ground. So I think that is the key. When the ball taker comes to ground, one defender only goes forward and grabs the ball carrier around shoulder height. You must face the same way as the ball carrier and use his momentum to pull him down or over your body, judo-style. It is easier if you drop in front of him. Some referees may penalise you, but they should not because it is just a tackle and it does not become a maul unless more than one defender is involved. The other forward defenders should quickly form after the tackle has been made and drive over the ball, attempting to create a turnover. If you are unsuccessful at stopping the formation of the maul, then it is time to bind and drive with commitment and purpose.

Some coaches are happy to commit just four forwards to push, and the other four are split two and two to either side, waiting for the break-away runners from the maul. This can work, but it is difficult to stand off and watch as your four defenders are retreating at a fast rate. Therefore, I think you should read the situation and commit more players if required. The scrum-half or halfback is in a good position to control this area and give instructions when necessary. Identify the strength of the threat and react accordingly. As earlier mentioned, some teams can set up a maul from a ruck or general play by quickly getting blocks in place and setting a solid base to stay on their feet. If one or two players peel off a ruck or a maul trying to set up another maul, a defender has two options:

- To quickly face the same way as the ball carrier and pull him to ground judo-style in the same way as mentioned in line-out defence, before the movement technically becomes a maul. The emphasis should be on getting it to ground.
- The other option as the first defender is to go in hard and high, trying to wrap up the attacker and sealing the ball. As the sole tackler after contact, you have every right to slide around to block the attacker from getting the ball back to his support. If you do this and your support arrives quickly to drive, there is a good chance of a turnover, on the use it or lose it rule. The supporting defenders must not come from the side, and only the first tackler can slide around to seal the ball.

TEAM ATTACK / TEAM DEFENCE

GAME-SENSE TRAINING, SEQUENCING, AND PLAYER EMPOWERMENT

What are team attack and team defence? The terms *team attack* and *team defence* refer to what players do in any given situation, no matter what position they play. For example, if a lock is at centre, can they read the situation correctly to make the right decision, either on attack or defence? There are many skills in the modern game that are generic, and all players need to have a good understanding of them. What is needed for successful team attack/defence?

- Positive attitude. The ability and confidence to make the best decision and take the best option.
- Player ownership. Players must believe in the concept and be empowered to take ownership.
- A good basic understanding of attack and defence options from all situations, e.g., set play, phase play, counterattack.
- Players of sufficient ability and skill to execute what is desired, e.g., decision making, scanning, communication, handling, understanding, etc.

What is game-sense training? You should create game-like activities where players are required to make decisions and choose options. Game-sense training uses games and activities as a learning tool to increase the motivation, the tactical and strategic thinking, and the skills of players. During game-sense activities, players are continually challenged to think about what they are doing and why they are doing it. This has many benefits, including promoting long-term learning, communication, teamwork, and leadership skills.

What is sequencing? Sequencing is the process of pre-planning phases to generate space or mismatches. They can be quite simple or very complex depending on the skill level of the players. Sequencing can be a valuable tool, but it must not be used as an exclusive method of coaching as it can be too regimented and can restrict flare and individualism. Sometimes you may find it difficult to perform your sequencing plays if the weather is not good.

What is player empowerment? Player empowerment is about giving the players the knowledge, understanding, skills, and ability to make the right decision at the right time in a game situation. For this to be achieved, coaches must set the guidelines but be flexible. Let players have an imput into team visons, season plans, game plans, etc. Encourage players to have input at trainings. Let players develop and expand on concepts with prompts from the coach. Encourage innovation and expansive thinking. Don't be critical of errors when they occur, and assist the players in correcting any problem. Give advice and feedback to the players, but do not be overbearing.

KEY POINTS

- Understanding the difference between spread and grouped defence and attack, and how they affect the way our players should react
- Undersanding the use of width and depth as an attacking weapon
- Understanding that the attacking options can often be created by the defensive team's formation and not always by the position you are on the field
- Though effective training, giving every player in the squad the skills and ability to fulfill any component of the game as required, within their individual limitations

FORWARD REQUIREMENTS

FORWARDS

- Win scrum and line-out—destroy and win opposition's ball
- Mobile to second phase
- High skill factor
- Body position
- Thinkers
- Aggressive defence
- Hard men that will not be intimidated

BACKS

- Decision makers
- Vision
- Confidence
- Pace
- Retention and delivery skills
- Attitude to attack
- Support
- Basic skills—mid-field kicking
- Defenders—aggression/thinkers

PERSONAL QUALITIES FOR ALL PLAYERS

- Will to succeed
- Desire
- Standards—team ethos
- Honesty
- Responsibility
- Ability to be accountable

LOCKS

- Size and bulk
- Coordinated
- Never give in
- Strong scrummagers
- Mobile
- Good tacklers
- Body position
- Good ball skills
- Explosive spring
- Hard-nosed, ruthless, be able to intimidate

TIGHTHEAD PROP

- Strong scrummager (massive strength)
- Mental hardness
- Resilient
- Good co-ordination (especially at line-outs)
- Mobile
- Tackler
- Lead the scrum — "the main man"
- Communicator

LOOSEHEAD PROP

- Mobility
- Explosive power
- Line-out ability
- Energy/enthusiasm (must get into the game)
- Ball skills — runner
- Body position
- Stay on feet

NUMBER EIGHT

- Ball skills and passing and catching
- Hardness — ability to take ball up

- Speed to manipulate blindside or open side
- Strong defence
- Vision
- Ability to go back
- Catching and kicking skills
- Line-out ability

BLINDSIDE FLANKER

- Size
- Line-out ability
- Speed off the mark
- Ball skills – good hands (receiver)
- Accuracy – defence and attack
- Aggressive defender
- Thinker
- Courageous – hard
- Body position vital
- Communicator (with wings defence)
- Needs to be able to anticipate
- Power, strong runner

OPEN-SIDE FLANKER

- Genuine speed
- Ball skills – distribution
- Ability to stay on his feet/win ball on the ground
- Effective communicator
- Intelligent – lines/moves
- Excellent tackler
- Vision
- Body position
- Tenacious
- Support and link
- Line-out option

HOOKERS

- Strong scrummager
- Pin-point throwing
- Mobility
- Urgency
- Accurate aggressive defender
- Thinker
- Vision
- Hard/non-compromising

RESERVES (PRINCIPLES)

- Versatility
- Team orientation (wants to play)
- Impact—adds value
- Must be good enough for the position
- Pushes always to get into team
- Encourages/positive/supportive

BASIC CONTINUITY
SKILLS SUMMARY

Continuity skills are position generic, i.e., every player on the field will be required to use them. Therefore, they need to understand them fully to carry them out. As a coach ask yourself these questions:

- How many scrums and line-outs are there in a game of rugby?
- How much time is spent practising these two phases of play?
- How clearly defined are the individual roles within them?

Now ask yourself:

- How many times is the ball taken into a contact situation in a game of rugby?
- How much time is spent practising these skills?

TAKING THE BALL INTO CONTACT:
PRE-CONTACT AND AT CONTACT

KEY FACTORS

- Focus on contact zone of opponent
- Chin off chest, eyes open
- Ball in two hands
- Low body position
- Body before ball
- Small steps on approach

OBJECTIVES

- To engage opposition

- To maintain possession
- To give teammates time and opportunity to support

Coaching Points

- The ball carrier is the "determinator" of ball retention at contact. This person will have the single greatest influence on ball retention.
- They must effectively shield ball from opponents by positioning ball away from contacts.
- Low body position and power step increases force and stability of contact.
- Every player on the field will take ball into contact; therefore, every player must understand and be competent in the key factors of this skill.
- The contact option, if taken, must be more advantageous than continuing the passing movement. Setting a target for support is not the only option when taking the ball into contact.
- Other options include: Hit, go to ground; hit and spin; hit and pass.

Common Mistakes

- Too upright at contact
- Narrow base of support at contact, causing instability
- Front foot planted too far from defender
- Too frontal at contact
- Shoulders below hips

Taking the Ball into Contact: Post-Contact (Standing in Tackle)

Key Factors

- Focus on contact area
- Chin off chest, eyes open
- Low body position

- Ball in two hands, away from contact
- Small steps on approach
- Wide "power step" into contact
- Plant front foot close to defender's feet
- Body before ball
- Contact side-on with hard parts of body, "jack up on contact"
- Maintain low, stable base, chin up, eyes open
- Hold ball in close at hip height
- Brace for impact (from defence and support)
- Transfer ball after initial contact and forward movement

OBJECTIVES
- To retain possession while engaging opposition
- To set effective target for supporting players, or utilize options created by support players

KEY WORDS
- Safety
- Protect ball
- Power step
- Contact
- Present target
- Transfer ball

COACHING POINTS
- The ball carrier is the key "determinator" of ball retention in contact.
- Once the ball carrier has assessed that passing is not the best option, the player should attempt to stand in the tackle.
- Ball carrier must retain "ownership" and responsibility for maintaining possession. Large numbers of turnover occur in the transfer from ball carrier to support.

- Ball carrier will dictate height of the supporting drive by the height at which they hold the ball.
- "Jack-up" refers to moving from a low to a high position on contact to unbalance tackler.
- Hard parts of body are shoulders, hips.

COMMON MISTAKES
- Head down, eyes closed
- Leading with ball
- Too upright
- Narrow base of support
- Front foot planted too far from defender's feet—easily taken to ground
- Shoulders below hips
- Holding ball in one hand
- Ball carrier failing to turn and give support a target to drive on
- Holding ball too high means support cannot effectively drive on

TAKING THE BALL INTO CONTACT: POST-CONTACT (ON THE GROUND)

KEY FACTORS
- Focus on contact area
- Chin off chest, eyes open
- Low body position
- Ball in two hands away from contact
- Small steps on approach to impact
- Body before ball
- Use power step to impact and continue forward movement
- Contact side-on with hard parts
- Strong leg drive forward before going to ground

- Immediately place ball to side of body toward your support and release
- Body at right angles to touchline

OBJECTIVES
- To engage opposition
- To retain possession
- To set effective target for supporting players

KEY WORDS
- Safety
- Protect ball
- Power step
- Drive forward
- Plant and release
- Get to feet
- Common errors

COACHING POINTS
- The longer you stay on your feet moving forward, the more defenders you will commit, thus creating space elsewhere.
- When falling to ground, tuck shoulder and roll with the impact.
- The ball must be placed or passed immediately, giving advantage to attacking team.
- Once the ball is released, the player cannot become involved in play in any way until they have retained their feet.
- Ball can be passed to support immediately from ground in tackle situation.
- Regain feet and join play as quickly as possible.

COMMON MISTAKES
- Ball carrier leading with ball
- Body position too high—easily turned toward opposition

- Going to ground too early
- Poor presentation of ball to support
- Playing ball or interfering with play while still on ground

TAKING THE BALL INTO CONTACT: POST-CONTACT (HIT AND SPIN)

KEY FACTORS

- Focus on contact area
- Chin off chest, eyes open
- Low body position
- Ball in two hands away from contact
- Small steps on approach
- Wide "power step" into contact
- Plant front foot close to defender's feet
- Body before ball
- Target to side of defender's shoulder
- Contact side-on, with hard parts, and spin to the outside of the shoulder contacted, maintaining momentum
- Burst away once facing forward

OBJECTIVES

- To engage opponent
- To spin off to maintain momentum
- To continue forward movement

KEY WORDS

- Safety
- Protect ball
- Hit
- Spin
- Burst away

Coaching Points

- To maintain momentum, ball carrier must target one side of defender (left shoulder of ball carrier to right side of defender and vice versa), aiming for controlled "ricochet" off, continuing forward.
- Ball security is paramount.

Common Mistakes

- Leading with the ball
- Contacting centre of defender, stopping forward momentum
- Spinning wrong way, presenting ball to defending team

PLANNING THE YEAR AHEAD

Decide what ingredients you require from players to construct your team combination from available player resources. Once identified, these ingredients must be part of the plan. By this I mean that they must be part of the agreement, so that players know what they must do to help the team achieve the short-term goals, which lead to the long-term aim.

AIM. To win the banner.

SHORT TERM GOALS. You can win within a game or have wins throughout the season, but not necessarily win a trophy. You can still create opportunities for high self-esteem.

Remember: Doing things slowly is perhaps the best way. Innovation and sharing problems will help you get results, rather than battling on your own.

Another important point is to *be honest*. Don't try to be someone else. You will always be found out. Never lie to a player or coach. Instead, tell it straight.

MANAGEMENT

The management team is very important. Numbers can vary, but you must have each individual in the management team committed and they must agree on a plan. There can be no hidden agendas.

MATERIAL RESOURCES

Equipment: scrum machine, ruck machine, tackle bags, good rugby balls, good training surface, safe area. Train in daylight when possible.

MANAGEMENT ADVICE

Words and ideas to remember: physical fitness, medical support, physio, strapper/masseur, adviser to assist in mental preparation, goal setting, anxiety control, focusing, diet advice, and personal development personnel.

Once you have the team available, it is important you outline the plan. Make sure the senior players, players' committee, captain, vice captain one, and vice captain two agree with what you are trying to achieve.

Start off slowly. In other words, keep going to the right, moving to the agreed zone, so that the locks always know where they are going. Keep going the same way or keep the target-setting basic.

Obviously, playing to the team's strengths is a temptation, but it is imperative to team build. Get the whole unit contributing, no matter how humble the player is. You want to get each player giving 100% of his energy, skill level, and concentration.

If you join those energy resources with a realistic plan, success will come!

PRACTICES

Practices must be organised. Plan well and stick to set times. It would be unrealistic to achieve excellence in a short time.

Tell your players what you want to achieve during training at the start. Have your tasks written down, like a shopping card.

Remember that fatigue reduces thinking levels and skill levels fail. Do the things that require accuracy early in the training, and the fatigue work at the end. But there must be reasons for the close proximity at the end of training.

Structure your training to involve the whole squad. Focus on communication and team work. Have a commitment to aim for mistake-free activity.

For safety at scrum practice, use resource people to cure problems.

Tackling practice is a very important part of team preparation. Discuss discipline, speed, technique, pain, and team bonding.

RULES

You must decide what the rules are. Players must know what fitness level they have to achieve.

The player must know he will be put on the line and will be compared to his peers. Encourage players to have training partners. Use resource people.

Set practice times. Obviously, try to suit the majority. Decide on time schedules, i.e., practice Tuesday for one and a half hours, and on Thursday for seventy minutes.

At the start of practice, assemble your players. Spell out what you want to achieve and what problems need to be rectified.

Share the tasks at practice, i.e., trainer takes the warm-up excercises, someone else is responsible for equipment, another calls the fatigue. Share the voice-load.

Set agreed in-house disciplinary procedures. The team must be a part of this decision-making process. Be realistic.

SET POLICIES

- Kickoff restarts. For receiving from halfway, and from the twenty-two. Ensure each player knows his role and test him on this. Don't let anyone be confused.
- Set scrums, moves, right hand up, left side up.
- Clear calls. Ensure locks and props know where they are going to be heading

USE KEY WORDS

- Line-outs, normal, shorts. Again ensure every player knows his job, i.e., blocking, lifting, leaping, safety valve.
- Defence. Keep rules simple, i.e., man-on-man, man, out drift.
- Discuss things again, as every member in the squad must be part of the defence.
- Setting targets. Discuss various options, why we set them.
- Discuss and explain "the rule," which is, "Eyes on the opponent all the time and don't ball watch."

TAP MOVES

Set a simple policy. What is the objective you want to achieve?

Decide on runners and support players' roles. Discuss ball retention. Negate 50/50 ball. Prevent opponents from getting a crack at the ball.

Discuss player commitment, especially at point-scoring time. Discuss players going to deck and supporting players blowing over.

Discuss the purpose of laying the ball up, so the halfback or designated scooper has a fair crack at the ball, so the ball can be spread or put into a protected environment for retention and eventually spread, testing the opposition's tacklers.

KICKING GAME

What is going to be the policy risk factor? Do you want to kick it out and compete on the throw in? It is better to turn over the ball through a deep kick that goes out and have a organised defence, than to turn the ball over with a disorganised defence?

Discuss counterattack.

Discuss kicking to the corners or down the tram lines. Discuss using second five or centre-kicking wipers, and why you are doing it.

Again, have clear, concise calls. Discuss ball height so specific chasers can apply pressure to receivers. The objective is to force them to kick out if they are caught in possession.

How do we beat a drift defence or man-out defence? Discuss cut-backs, grubber kicks, forty-five-degree runners.

ON-FIELD DISCIPLINE

- Rucking
- Responsibility to referee
- Responsibility to team members
- Policy of the protectors, keeping the ball up as an option, hence retaining possession for as long as possible
- Showing the ball at the back of maul, so referee and halfback share communication, hence retain ball
- Discuss pre-match build up
- Forwards and backs meetings?
- Discuss policy concerning injuries and players recovering, such as concussions, bruising, bones, icing, stretching, cuts, etc.
- Friday night and Saturday morning diet, food intake after performance

CREATING SPACE

There are many play situations using various types of passes and running of lines that can be used to create space. Coaches are only limited by their own imagination in the use of these in a game. The success of any of these plays will depend on the coach's ability to coach them to the players and the amount of time and quality performance applied in a coaching session.

The principle role of a football carrier in attack is to progress the football up field until reaching a situation where this is no longer possible. Their responsibility is then to endeavour to create a gap or space for support players to continue the go-forward attack. In creating space, the ball carrier must effectively ensure that any prospective defenders are drawn away from the support player who can run into the created space or gap. This space may only be small, maybe one metre wide or perhaps a greater distance between two defending players.

In creating these situations, players must first be proficient in all skill techniques necessary. Primarily, the aim is to create a situation of having more attacking players than defenders, e.g., two attacking players against one defender.

A player's ability to create space will depend on:
• Individual skill level
• Vision
• Understanding of the situation
• Judgement
• Timing (running and passing)

There are three basic abilities to look at:
1. Draw and pass
2. Run angles
3. Unders and overs

Let's look at those in detail.

DRAW AND PASS

This is probably the most basic skill that can be used to create space, but it is the end product of a number of well-coordinated movement patterns as well as judgement and timing. It is a well-executed skill designed to create space for support players to run into and is mostly used in orthodox attacking play and one-on-one defence.

Effectiveness of this skill depends on players ability to:
- Skillfully execute all movements of the running and passing techniques
- To judge how and when to commit a defender
- Time a pass, and what the support players' positions are
- Assess actions of all positions directly involved
- Use vision
- Communicate

RUN ANGLES

Changing the point of attack by changing the angle through the ball carrier and support player creates space effectively.

The success of this play requires:
- Refined ball handling and passing skill
- Judgement
- Timing—running and passing
- Running lines of both players
- Decision making of when to change angle
- Communication
- Vision

The illustrated drill is aimed at creating space back on the inside of the defender for the support player.

Attacking ball carrier A must create the space by running toward the defender D1, then at the appropriate moment with good footwork change angle to defender D2, making sure that both defenders are committed to tackle A.

Support player S using judgement and timing runs forward, then changes angle back inside D1 to make use of created space.

ANGLES

SETTING: Grid 10 x 15m, 4 markers, 8-16 players, one football for each "A" player.

Make certain that when the S player receives the ball from A he is out of range of D1 and his early vision.

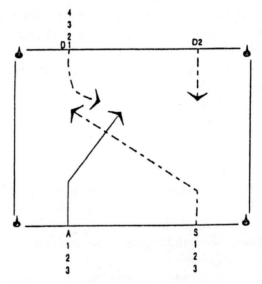

- A runs out and cuts across the grid to draw D so that D cannot take S.
- S moves out on a straight line, angles back to cut in behind Al.

- S times his run to occur when A has drawn D and runs as close to A as possible without being tackled by D.

ROTATION: S to D1, A to D2, D1 to S, D2 to A

UNDERS AND OVERS

In both plays, the aim of the ball carrier is to create space for support player from a situation of having equal number of attacking and defending players.

This might be best explained in the drills provided, but the responsibility and success of the play will depend initially on the ball carrier whose best line of running is straight on to a defender to commit that defender before suddenly changing the angle of run through good footwork and delivering a good pass to a support player who has timed the run to the correct position.

The success of these plays depends on both the ball carrier and the support player understanding their roles and having the correct techniques to create all of the movements.

The successful performance of these plays will depend on players having the advanced skills and ability to read and understand the action and reaction of all involved.

UNDERS PLAY

SETTING: Grid 10 x 10m, 4 markers, 8-16 players, 1 football for each A player.

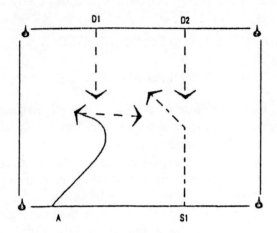

- A leads out and moves inside D1.
- A passes the ball under D1.
- S leaves the straight line of run and D2, cutting into the gap between D1 and D2.

ROTATION: S (with ball) to A, A to D1, D1 to D2, D2 to S

COACHING POINTS

Through good passing and drawing technique attack A runs a line to commit defender Dl. With D1 committed, A takes the step away, ensuring D1 follows across. At the correct time, support S1 will change angle and run into space between D1 and defender D2 and receive a pass from A. S1 angles in behind D1 to get behind the defence line and then immediately straightens his run.

Essentials are:
- Good techniques
- Judgement
- Timing
- Vision
- Reading play

OVERS PLAY

SETTING: Grid 1.0 x 10m, 4 markers, 3–16 players, 1 football for each A player.

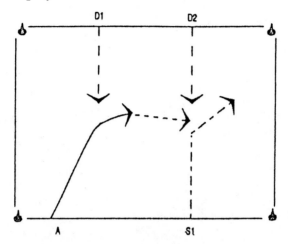

- A leads out and cuts across D1.
- A passes over D1 and D2 to S1.
- S leaves the straight line of run, and D2 moves outside of D2.

ROTATION: S (with ball) to A, A to D1, D1 to D2, D2 to S

COACHING POINTS

Attacking player A runs a line to D1's right shoulder to commit D1, then changes angle across and runs a line to commit defender D2 and draws him away from support player S1, thus creating space on the outside. S1 runs straight and then changes angle away from D2 at the appropriate time and receives a pass to take advantage of created space outside of D2.

Development and refinement of all the evasive techniques and plays are achieved by quality coaching in drill and play situations. As players practice and become more skillful, the components of judgement, timing, anticipation, and reading play will be developed in conjunction with the physical movement pattern. It is only when all of these components are mastered that players will have the confidence to apply their skills during the game.

CATCHING

HIGH KICK

First of all, be relaxed and confident. Next, focus on the ball and pick its line of flight. Use small steps to get under the ball. Stand side-on so if you drop the ball, it will not be knocked forward. This also puts you in to a stronger position for contact, with your bigger muscle groups being on the sides of your body. Raise your arms above your head to meet the ball before bringing it down to your chest. If you try to catch the ball with your arms below eye level, your elbows tend to stay out too far and your chances of dropping the ball are increased. Also, if the ball is floating around a little, it can shift during the split second it takes to fall from above your head down to your hands while unsighted. So always keep your hands and arms up.

RECEIVING THE PASS

Once again, keep your hands up with fingers wide apart. Your thumbs should be pointed back towards you, with arms semi-stretched in the direction of where the ball is coming from. This gives a good target for the passer of the ball to aim at with confidence. It is very important for the catcher to hold the depth and not be too flat, which may encourage a forward pass. Call loud and clear for the ball, and an accurate pass is more likely. Plus, your chances of getting the ball are increased. Another important habit to get into as a receiver is to turn your upper body into the direction of where the ball is coming from. This gives you your entire chest to take a hard pass, or if the ball slips through your fingers, your chest is a good back-up. Too many players are already running away from the pass before the ball has been taken cleanly. In doing this, the chances of an error are dramatically increased.

When taking a pass, try to keep your hands flexible and subtle. Soft hands will help you catch and move the ball across your body to deliver a nice pass.

DEFENCE

Half the game of rugby is defence, but we don't spend anywhere near fifty percent of our training time on defence. Almost every year, the team with the best defensive record wins the competition. Former Australian rugby league coach Bobby Fulton would really emphasize the importance of good defence, and if his team defended well, he said the attack would take care of itself. His side, Manly, was the top team in 1996 with conceding an average of only nine points per game. Rugby Union is no different. The lateral defensive line has become similar in both codes.

From set play, I think one-out defence is the best way to go, with your flanker taking the number ten or the first cut back. So your ten marks twelve, twelve marks thirteen, and your thirteen marks their fifteen, who often comes in outside centre. It is still man-on-man defence, but you are not marking the guy with the same number on his back as you have.

The two most important aspects of all defence are communication and keeping your defensive line. As a line, you can slide across if necessary as the ball is shifted, even if you are outnumbered. You should defend inside your opponents, encouraging them to run across the field, which makes their attack less effective. Marking inside out also makes it easier to perform a good side-on shoulder tackle.

Good communication is essential so you can let each other know where you are and who you are marking. This will stop two defenders committing to the same attacker. As the first tackler, you should watch the attackers hips and try to pick the line of his run and get your body on that line, which will help you execute a strong tackle. Your body and shoulder, as opposed to just your arm, should be behind the tackle. Generally speaking, I like the first tackler to go low and stop the forward momentum, and the second tackler or assist can then go high, attacking the ball.

The Canterbury Crusaders encourage hitting on the up in the stomach and ribs department as these areas are soft compared with the defender's shoulder. If you can hit on the up and grab one leg at the same time, the attacker will be in a weak position off the ground.

You have to decide which tackle technique is required for each situation. The upper body tackle is fine if you are strong and have some forward momentum, but you should never lose sight of the low copybook tackle when the attacker has momentum up or is physically bigger than you are. They can not run without their legs, and too many young players these days are going in too high and getting brushed off.

One-out is the best for first-phase defence, but for second- and third-phase play, go back to man-on-man. Hopefully one of your forwards will be standing off so your backs can still defend one-out and there is no overlap. If there is no forward as the first defender, then I think your stand-off must stay in and mark their stand-off. The immediate danger is close to the ruck, and if the attack goes wide, hopefully you can still slide fast enough to cover the outside backs. Defence patterns are only a guide, and I think if anyone comes within one or two metres of you with the ball, then you have to take them regardless. Sometimes you come across teams who you know have big forwards and will play ten-man rugby against you. Be proactive and reactive to keep your defence close in, where the biggest threat lies. Tackle in twos if required. The same goes for a team who will attack wide — adjust your defence wider or tell everyone to take a step out. Your fullback should communicate and organise the defence to the danger zones.

Whichever form of tackle technique you choose, try to always finish on top of the attacker. This puts you in a good position to quickly regain your feet and pick up the ball. When performing a tackle assist, a good skill to learn is pulling the attacker down while remaining on your feet. As you are on your feet, you have all the rights when trying to recapture possession. I think you should then try to get one leg over the tackled player, preferably with your backside facing the opposition's support. Get into a triangle position, low with your feet wide apart. Having a wide stance with a low centre of gravity will put you in a strong position and help you to create a turnover.

Here are some tackle technique coaching tips.

FRONT-ON TACKLE

- Sight the target.
- Pre-tackle stance.
- Go forward.
- Contact shoulder on target.
- Lock on with arms.
- Power drive, finish on top.
- Regain feet and contest possession.

SIDE-ON TACKLE

- Sight target.
- Position inside ball carrier.
- Pre-tackle stance.
- Zero in on target.
- Drive with legs, contact with shoulder.
- Head behind attacker's body.
- Lock on with arms.
- Continue power drive.
- Regain feet, recover ball or realign.

When defending, don't ball-watch as the guy you are supposed to be marking may change his angle or position and catch you unaware of the line of his run.

Think positively and take up the challenge of every tackle with a tough mental attitude. My defensive self-talk before a game would consist of the following: if anyone wants to run at me, they do it at their peril, and if anyone runs into my zone, they will get smashed.

SPORTING BACKGROUND

I was lucky enough to be brought up in a strong sporting environment. My family is very well known in New Zealand through the sport of harness racing or horse racing. Both my grandfathers were the leading horse trainers of New Zealand in their time. Wes Butt was a seven-time champion, and Derek Jones was champion three times. In 2002, my elder brother, Anthony, became the youngest harness driver ever to win 1000 races in New Zealand. When I was twenty-two, I became the first person to be a back-to-back Australasian young drivers champion. I have also trained the winners of around seventy horse races and driven well over 100 winners, when not focused totally on rugby.

When driving horses in a race, your decision making has to be extremely accelerated and few sports can match the intensity required. Therefore, it has been an excellent introduction or grounding for me in sports. My father, Murray, has always been very supportive and positive when encouraging my rugby or horse racing. He is a good coach without realizing it. With harness racing, there are up to fifteen horses in a race with only one winner, so you learn how to react to not winning.

Sometimes you can not control the result, but you can always control your response. Every coach has tough times, so when you do, don't be non-responsive. There is an old saying that goes, "A smooth sea never made a skilful mariner." Expect hard times and expect the unexpected.

You can affect the present and future, but not the past. I admire former All Black captain Sean Fitzpatrick for the way he could be so competitive on the field, then as soon as the final whistle blew, his intensity would drop and he became a gentleman on TV, regardless of the result. Martin Johnson and Rubern Thorne have similar qualities. In the past I have heard the saying, "Winning is not everything; it is the only thing." This is macho bullshit in my opinion. What happens if you don't win? Do you jump off a cliff? Of-course not. This sort of talk only adds pressure. A good coach absorbs pressure and does not pass it on to his players. They would much rather receive reasons for why they are going to win. This will instill confidence and not anxiety. Most players at any level lack confidence. Sometimes you come across a player who has lots of confidence, which is no problem as long as they can keep their thoughts to themselves. Former Australian rugby league player and now boxer Anthony Mundine is a good example of this. He is an unbelievable talent, and I would love the players I coach to have his skill and confidence — but he would be far better off keeping it to himself, rather than making statements to the press that make him very unpopular with much of the general public. Many consider him too arrogant.

I think the British press has had a detrimental effect on the sporting success or lack of it in their country. The press, it seems, sometimes builds a player or athlete up then — once that player is a celebrity — looks to knock them for the sake of a news story. This does nothing to encourage young people who are interested in sports. In New Zealand, our British heritage sometimes comes through, and we can be too negative when results do not go our way. The nation's handling of the 1999 World Cup semi-final loss to France was an example of this when all the players were bagged and the coach was spat on when he went out in public. For God's sake, we are supposed to be a sporting nation. What sort of example is this to our children? Former All Black great and Italy coach John Kirwan once said that when he played for the All Blacks, they had a huge fear of losing (probably because of the public's reaction). He thought they would be better if they were instead motivated by the

116

joy of winning. We are sometimes too judgmental, and a lot of our children lack self-esteem because of peer-pressure. As a result, New Zealand has the highest rate of youth suicide in the world.

All children should be encouraged to participate in a sport of some kind. They should enjoy it, and sports should make their lives more fruitful. We all know that physical fitness is a problem in many countries, and sports are the answer to better health. Sports also help develop social skills and a good work ethic.

Do not have a win-at-all-cost attitude. Winning is not everything. It is, however, the ultimate reward. As a coach if you do not win and your team needs to be reprimanded, make sure the players know that it is not personal and you are talking about the performance. It is the performance that you are not happy with, and it needs to improve. The players are just as important to the team as they have always been, and you should try to finish on a positive note. Reinforcement is an art. After a loss, the ability of the coach and players to regroup and refocus is very important. It says a lot about your character. Former Canterbury and Wales coach Steve Hansen had a good after-match routine when he coached club rugby in Christchurch. At the after-match function, each player would join Hansen one at a time for a seven-ounce beer to discuss their game — a simple but effective communication activity.

Sometimes you come across players who were not competitive enough on the field. They should be hurting after a loss. If they are not then they are not trying hard enough or it doesn't mean enough to them, and they need to work hard if they want to succeed.

The most successful American football coach of all time, Don Shula, had a good system where he and his team had a twenty-four-hour period after each game to analyse their performance. If they won, they had a day to enjoy the victory, and if they lost, they had twenty-four hours to dwell on the game. After that time, it was team policy to refocus on the job at hand, which was the next week's game. Losing was serious but not fatal.

Coaching is so much about your interaction with your players. I think, generally speaking, that coaching is fifty percent knowledge of the game and fifty percent people skills.

In closing, you will reach your goals if you are willing to pay the price to get there. Go forward without fear.

ACKNOWLEDGEMENTS

I would like to acknowledge the following people: Suzanne Haws (Iceni Books), Lee Golding (Canterbury R.F.U.), Basil Bey (Rugby365.com), Leigh Ayers (Canterbury Netball), and Matt McIlraith (N.Z.R.F.U.).

Printed in the United Kingdom
by Lightning Source UK Ltd.
9799800001B/36